own your
Faith

THE ADVENTURE OF
FOLLOWING CHRIST IN COLLEGE

own your
faith

MARK TABB
FOREWORD BY STEPHEN BALDWIN

THINK

TH1NK
P.O. Box 35001
Colorado Springs, Colorado 80935

TH1NK is an imprint of NavPress.
TH1NK and the TH1NK logo are registered trademarks of NavPress. Absence of ® in connection with marks of NavPress or other parties does not indicate an absence of registration of those marks.

ISBN 13: 978-1-60006-097-7
ISBN 10: 1-60006-097-8

Cover design by BURNKIT
Cover image by BURNKIT
Creative Team: Nicci Hubert, Melanie Knox, Reagen Reed, Arvid Wallen, Pat Reinheimer

Tabb, Mark A.
   Own your faith : the adventure of following Christ in college / Mark Tabb.
      p. cm.
   Includes bibliographical references.
   ISBN 1-60006-097-8
   1. College students--Religious life. 2. Universities and colleges--Religion. I. Title.
   BV4531.3.T33 2007
   248.8'34--dc22
                                    2006034880
Printed in the United States of America

1 2 3 4 5 6 7 8 9 10 / 11 10 09 08 07

FOR BETHANY, HANNAH, AND SARAH

CONTENTS

FOREWORD

I launched my own ministry called Breakthrough. And yeah, the thought that Doyle from *Bio-Dome* would launch his own ministry strikes me as hilarious as well. Who but God would pick a nutcase like Stevie B to impact a generation in a new, innovative, and exciting way? And that's what the Breakthrough does. I like to tell people this ain't your grandma's ministry—unless your grandma rounded up a group of elite extreme sport athletes, packed them into arenas across the country, amped up the place with the best Christian rock and hip hop music, and watched as thousands of people came to Christ every night. That's the Breakthrough.

Like I said, this ain't your grandma's ministry.

And after reading *Own Your Faith* you will understand how you can't ride on your grandma's faith. Or you momma's. Or your daddy's. Or anyone else's. I didn't grow up as a Christian. Yeah, I believed in God, but I've come to understand that there is a big difference between believing in God and following Jesus. You can believe and stay pretty comfortable bouncing along with life. But when the Holy Spirit grabs hold of you, and you become a follower of Jesus, get ready. You're in for the ride of your life.

My wife became a Christian about a year before I did. For twelve straight months she got down on her face for an hour a day and prayed for me. At first I thought it was cute. Then I found it silly. Finally I figured out she was experiencing something real. And I wasn't. So I started checking this whole Jesus thing out. I started going to church with her, and I started asking questions. Once or twice I even prayed what is known as "the sinner's prayer." But it wasn't until I became willing to enter into this experience God's way, with nothing held back, that I discovered the truth of what it means to follow Jesus. No one could do this for me. I had to do it myself. I had to make my faith my own. My wife could pray for me for a solid year, but when push came to shove, she couldn't believe for me.

Right after I came to Christ, I struck a deal with God. Some deal. In my mind, I climbed up on top of the biggest, gnarliest-looking rock you can imagine, and I shook my fist at God. I told him that he better be real because he was about to get all of Stevie B with nothing held back. As dramatic as that moment felt, it was only the beginning. In this experience I'm having with Jesus, I've found that I need to continually renew my mind by reading his Word, the Bible. People challenge me all the time on what I say I believe, so I had to learn to think like Jesus. And I had to get my hands dirty serving people. No one had to push me to do that.

I believe God is raising up a new generation in an uprising of faith that is going to blow away everything that came before. I don't know about you, but I don't want to miss out. But you won't get to be a part of the uprising until you are ready to become a gnarly, hardcore follower of Christ yourself. You've got to make your faith your own. Mark Tabb's latest book is a good place to start.

Stephen Baldwin

ACKNOWLEDGMENTS

I WOULD LIKE TO THANK Nicci Hubert for asking me to tackle this project and for her encouragement along the way. Thank you as well to Melanie Knox, Reagen Reed, and the rest of the editorial team at NavPress. I appreciate their hard work, dedication, and patience. Finally, I would like to thank Troy Doubman, Tony Manning, Rusty Kennedy, and especially my three daughters for their input into this project. Their answers to my many, many questions helped shape this book and pushed me in directions I would never have tried on my own.

WHOSE FAITH
DO YOU HAVE?

CHAPTER 1

A DAY MAY COME, if it hasn't already, when you will walk into your room and feel like a stranger. Looking around at the posters on the walls and the CDs on a shelf and the letterman's jacket lying on the floor, you realize that none of it fits. This isn't you — at least, not anymore. Maybe it never was. You stick what was once your favorite CD into your CD player. Before the first song is over, you pull the CD out and say to yourself, "I can't believe I used to like this stuff." That's why you never loaded it into your iPod, yet you could never bring yourself to throw it out. That band serenaded some good times in your life, but it hasn't for a while. On this day you realize it never will again.

You've been through this before. There was that day you realized Barney was lame and the day you gave all your Barbies to your little sister. Somewhere along the way you stopped collecting action figures, and a McDonald's Happy Meal no longer struck you as fine dining. You exchanged chocolate milk for Starbucks and The Disney Channel for *Seinfeld*. Those moments may not have felt like turning points, but they were. It's not that you became too old for those things that used to matter so much to you. You simply outgrew them. Intellectually. Emotionally. Even spiritually. You moved on with life, and as you did, some things had to be left behind. Most of the time you didn't make conscious decisions about what to take with you and what to box up for Goodwill. One day you woke up and you had changed. The act of living out the new you made those decisions for you.

WHEN THE PIECES DON'T FIT   The stuff you accumulated in your room during your first eighteen years of life is not the only thing that no longer fits. The more you learn about yourself, the more you will find that many of the odd collection of ideas and beliefs rolling around in your head now seem strangely out of place. Just like the concert T-shirts piled up on a shelf in your closet, not all your old beliefs still fit who you are today. As you try them on, you realize some are like that crush on the Olsen twins or Aaron Carter you had in the ninth grade. They made a lot of sense at the time, but you find them a little embarrassing today.

Other ideas you've collected pose a greater challenge. From the day you popped out of the womb, your parents, other influential adults, and peers filled your head with ideas about the world. They shaped your concept of right and wrong, as well as your understanding of truth. When you are very young, even your likes and dislikes are extensions of your parents'. That's why in 1968 I became a tireless neighborhood campaign worker for Richard Nixon. I was six years old. My dad took me to see Nixon during a campaign stop at a local airport, and I was hooked. In my little six-year-old brain, I believed Richard Millhouse Nixon would be the greatest president since Abraham Lincoln. I was the youngest of the young Republicans in my hometown, and Nixon was my guy.

In spite of the Nixon wristwatch I bought at the end of his

first term (a watch I still own today, although I'm not exactly sure where it is at the moment), Nixon wasn't really my candidate. My attachment to him was nothing more than an extension of my father's political beliefs. If I'd never grown beyond this point, I would still need to call my dad before every election to find out who he plans to vote for. I could have just as easily gone to the opposite extreme and hated Nixon because my dad loved him, but that wouldn't have been much of an improvement. My political convictions still wouldn't be my own. They would simply be some sort of Bizarro-world version of my father's.

Political ideas are minor in comparison to an even more important set of beliefs you picked up as you were growing up: your beliefs about God. As you go off to college and get out on your own for the first time, you will most likely find yourself sorting through these beliefs, trying to decide which fit the real you. More than that, you have to figure out if God and Jesus and the Bible are truly your own or if your convictions are nothing more than extensions of the faith of the strong Christians in your life. The real question you have to ask yourself is this: *Whose Jesus do I have? Is he mine, or do I believe because others believe?*

And that's where this book comes in. As the title says, the goal of this book is to help you take full ownership of your faith, to make Jesus completely your own. I don't want this book to be another crutch that tells you what to believe and why. Instead, I want to help you discover an honest, gritty, real faith that springs out of a relationship you share with God alone. Don't get me wrong. We all need others to help us get started and keep growing with Jesus. However, there comes a point in our spiritual development when we can't depend on others for answers. Otherwise we will end up like the seven sons of Sceva in Acts 19:13-16 who went around casting out demons by saying, "I command you by the Jesus preached by Paul!" One day they ran into a real evil spirit who shot back, "I know Jesus and I've heard of Paul, but who are you?" Sceva's seven sons barely escaped with their lives after the possessed man turned on them. Piggybacking on the faith of others may work for a while, but eventually Jesus has to become truly our own if our faith is to survive.

TESTS ARE COMING   I'd originally planned to make this next section a clever relationship quiz that dripped with sarcastic humor to help you figure out where you stand with God. But the quiz ended up on the cutting-room floor, because I realized quizzes about your relationship with God are about as effective as a quiz in some teen magazine that is supposed to help you figure out if the guy you are dating is Mr. Right or if you are your girlfriend's soul mate. Those quizzes usually give you the answer you wanted to find in the first place. The same goes for a God relationship quiz. Some of you would read a question that asks, "Do you pray enough?" and automatically say "no," even if you'd just spent the past three days lying on your face pouring out your heart to God. And others would say "yes, of course," even if in the past six months you hadn't prayed for anything more significant than answers on a physics test you forgot to study for.

Maybe that's why the Bible doesn't include any relationship quizzes. That omission, however, shouldn't lead us to jump to the conclusion that God never tests us and our relationship with him. He does. Daily. The questions, however, aren't written out in black and white with convenient "yes" and "no" boxes for us to check. Instead, God allows our faith to be tested in ways that probe the very core of our convictions. Jesus described this process in one of his most famous stories:

> "A farmer planted seed. As he scattered the seed, some of it fell on the road and birds ate it. Some fell in the gravel; it sprouted quickly but didn't put down roots, so when the sun came up it withered just as quickly. Some fell in the weeds; as it came up, it was strangled among the weeds and nothing came of it. Some fell on good earth and came up with a flourish, producing a harvest exceeding his wildest dreams." (Mark 4:3-8)

If your first response to reading this is, "What does a farmer planting seeds have to do with my relationship with God?" you are in good company. Jesus' disciples didn't get it at first, either. That's why Jesus had to spell it out for them and us. He explained the story of the farmer by telling his disciples:

> "The farmer plants the Word. Some people are like the seed that falls on the hardened soil of the road. No sooner do they hear the Word than Satan snatches away what has been planted in them.
>
> "And some are like the seed that lands in the gravel. When they first hear the Word, they respond with great enthusiasm. But there is such shallow soil of character that when the emotions wear off and some difficulty arrives, there is nothing to show for it.
>
> "The seed cast in the weeds represents the ones who hear the kingdom news but are overwhelmed with worries about all the things they have to do and all the things they want to get. The stress strangles what they heard, and nothing comes of it.

"But the seed planted in the good earth represents those who hear the Word, embrace it, and produce a harvest beyond their wildest dreams." (Mark 4:14-20)

God allows birds and rocks and thorns to come into our lives to check out our faith and determine not only whether or not it is real, but if it is our own. It's not like this will be a completely new experience for you. If you were an active follower of Christ in your high school, you've already encountered some rocks and thorns. However, the challenges you'll face in college take these tests to a whole different level. God isn't being cruel by letting this happen. Far from it. His goal is to help you grow up and become fully mature in your faith, and that can't happen as long as your beliefs, convictions, and behaviors are extensions of those of your parents or your youth pastor or your Christian girlfriend. You will discover whose Jesus you have as God allows into your life some unique tests, which you can only experience through the phase of life you are about to enter. These tests include:

1. Your parents aren't there to watch over you.

Moving off to college can be like living at Outback Steakhouse (without the steaks and Bloomin' Onions and anything else that approaches edible food): "No Rules. Just Right." Of course there are a few rules. All colleges have rules against under-age drinking and the use of illegal substances. Christian colleges go further by limiting when guys can go into girls' dorms or floors and vice versa. But, for the most part, you are on your own; no one is standing over you telling you what to do, and no one is there to make sure you do the right thing. Your mom and dad don't know what you are up to unless you tell them.

Go ahead and insert your own story about that friend whose

parents were really strict and who became a hellion the moment he or she went off to college. This nice kid, who never did anything wrong throughout high school, landed on a college campus and started drinking and partying and sleeping around—basically became his or her parents' worst nightmare, if the parents even knew what was going on. I knew people like this when I was in school, and you probably do as well.

What causes Christians like this to go off the deep end? It wasn't just that they couldn't handle the peer pressure of college. The real problem came down to this: Jesus wasn't their own. They kept the rules because their parents made them keep the rules. Imitating Christ wasn't something that welled up from deep within their own souls. That's the purpose of this test, to see whether or not Jesus has truly transformed your life, or if you toe the line because that's what's expected of you.

2. Your old support system didn't move with you.

Living for Jesus in high school is no easy task. To make it, most of us have to develop some sort of support system. You have your Christian friends at school and your youth group at church, complete with a youth pastor or other adults who help you stick with Christ. Usually you have other adults as well: parents, pastors, neighbors—people who genuinely care for you and try to mentor you in the faith.

Then you move off to college, but your support system doesn't move with you. Even if you go to a school close to home or live at home and commute, things will change. Those buddies you hung out with, who shared your desire to stay close to God? You don't see them every day like you once did. Your lives start going in different directions. Now what will you do? How will your faith survive when you find you can't lean on the people you once leaned on? It's times like this, when it's just you and God, that he looks at you and asks, "Am I enough for you?"

3. Temptation surrounds you.

We interrupt this book for a special message from parents everywhere: College can be scary. People at college like to do bad things. They will try to get you to do bad things, too. This is called temptation. Beware of temptation. Temptation bad. Resisting temptation good. And now we return to our regularly scheduled programming. . . .

Okay, it's not like you've never faced temptation before. Sex. Drugs. Alcohol. More sex, drugs, and alcohol. You've had to face these temptations since junior high. Maybe earlier. However, the question you must come to grips with is no longer, will you drink or have sex or do whatever. The real question becomes, *why* will you choose to either give in or walk away. In God's eyes, what you do means far less than why you do it. And the question of why is something you are now going to have to figure out in a way you never have before.

4. Beliefs and truths you've always taken for granted will be called into question.

And they need to be.

Yes, you read it right. Our beliefs and our concepts of truth need to be called into question. You need professors who will shake the foundations of your faith. You need to get to know students who will make you wonder if there really is a difference between Christianity and Islam. And you need to read books that make you question whether you can really know anything at all. You need all of this. Yes, you *need* it. We all need it. Your profs and friends and books aren't playing into the hands of the

Devil to shipwreck your faith. Honestly, they aren't doing anything God himself doesn't do. Read through the first four books of the New Testament and note how many times Jesus made his disciples' heads spin. How many times did he tell people to leave if they couldn't handle what he had to say? The answer: a bunch.

I know, I know, it's bad when someone's faith is shipwrecked. But, shipwrecks happen because ships sail across the ocean. The only surefire way to avoid a shipwreck is to never put your boat in the water. And the only surefire way to keep your faith safe and sound and never question anything, ever, for your entire life is to stay cooped up in some safe little Christian cocoon, where nothing bad will ever happen to you, and no one will ever plant a seed of doubt in your head. Of course, you will then be about as useful to God as a ship in perpetual dry dock.

5. Oh yeah, did I mention the Devil has us in his crosshairs?

People make a lot of jokes about hell and the Devil. He also shows up in movies as the ultimate big bad wolf that even Schwarzenegger has trouble defeating. But this is no joking matter, and it isn't the stuff of movies. Satan, the Devil, is a real being, and he never stops trying to ruin your testimony and make you completely unusable to God. He does more than tempt you to break as many of the Ten Commandments as possible. His real goal is to separate you from God and God's eternal plan for your life. And he never rests.

Just because Jesus already defeated the Devil doesn't mean Satan will now leave you alone. However, Jesus' victory gives you the weapons and confidence you need as you make your way in this world. Paul said it best:

God is strong, and he wants you strong. So take everything the Master has set out for you, well-made weapons
of the best materials. And put them to use so you will
be able to stand up to everything the Devil throws your
way. This is no afternoon athletic contest that we'll walk
away from and forget about in a couple of hours. This is
for keeps, a life-or-death fight to the finish against the
Devil and all his angels.

Be prepared. You're up against far more than you can
handle on your own. Take all the help you can get, every
weapon God has issued, so that when it's all over but the
shouting you'll still be on your feet. Truth, righteousness,
peace, faith, and salvation are more than words. Learn
how to apply them. You'll need them throughout your
life. God's Word is an *indispensable* weapon. In the same
way, prayer is essential in this ongoing warfare. Pray
hard and long. Pray for your brothers and sisters. Keep
your eyes open. Keep each other's spirits up so that no
one falls behind or drops out. (Ephesians 6:10-18)

~

Jesus said birds will come and snatch away the word of truth
from the lives of some. Others will be done in by thorns or shal-
low soil. But these are risks we have to be willing to face head-
on. Unlike seeds lying on the ground, no one can snatch your
faith from you unless you let them. Working through the process
of making your faith your own will bury those seeds of truth
deep within you, even as you wrestle with hard questions, never-
before-considered concepts, and ideas thrown at you by atheist
friends and professors. As James wrote,

Consider it a sheer gift, friends, when tests and challenges come at you from all sides. You know that under pressure, your faith-life is forced into the open and shows its true colors. So don't try to get out of anything prematurely. Let it do its work so you become mature and well-developed, not deficient in any way. (James 1:2-4)

When you know tests are coming, it is best to prepare yourself in advance, the same way you'll be preparing for your first political science exam. And the best place to start is coming to grips with what this faith is all about.

SECTION 1

know

THE SHORTEST DISTANCE

CHAPTER 2

THE SHORTEST DISTANCE BETWEEN two points is a straight line. It's been a long time since I took geometry, but I remember this little rule. When I book a flight from Indianapolis to New York, I always choose the airline that flies straight there, rather than one that goes through Chicago or Detroit or Miami. Call me crazy, but I don't see much point in flying an extra 1,800 miles and quadrupling my travel time if I don't have to. The direct route is always the best route.

THE SHORTEST DISTANCE TO GOD The direct route to God is also the best route. There was a time when the direct route was not available to everyone. The Old Testament records that no one could go straight to God except the priests, and even then there were no guarantees that God would let them get near him. Once a year the high priest would take the blood of a sacrifice into the most holy place in the temple and sprinkle it on the mercy seat on top of the ark of the covenant. (The most holy place was the place where God's Spirit dwelt and the place where the priests made atonement for the sins of the nation.) However, the priests who went inside didn't always make it out alive. If they tried to enter God's presence with hidden sins in their lives, God's overwhelming holiness would stop them dead in their tracks. Because of the potential deadly consequences of approaching God Almighty, the priests had bells sewn on the hems of their robes and tied a rope around one ankle when they went into the holy place. The other priests listened for the ringing of the bells. If the bells stopped ringing, they would drag the guy's dead body out with the rope.

Believe it or not, this was the only path to God available until Jesus came to earth. When he died for our sins and rose from the grave, he threw open the doors to his Father's house for us. He now tells us we can "walk right up to him and get what he is so ready to give. Take the mercy, accept the help" (Hebrews 4:16). No longer do we have to go through intermediaries. Because Jesus intercedes for us with his Father, we have direct access to God, a straight-line path that the heroes of the Old Testament could only dream of.

THE POINT OF THIS WHOLE ENDEAVOR You may be reading this and thinking to yourself, *Yeah, so what? I'm a Christian. I know all of this already*, and you probably do. However, knowing and doing are two different things. If you've spent much time in churches, you've already heard how the Christian life is all about a *personal relationship with Christ*. Those last four words are thrown around in church circles so often that they've become an ingrained part of the Christian vocabulary. Instead of asking someone if they are a Christian, we ask, "Do you have a *personal relationship with Christ*?" During my years as a pastor, I used this phrase over and over, week after week. I would tell people how Christ died and rose again so that we can have a *personal* *relationship with him.* That's the way Christ followers talk. The words are burned into our psyches.

However, I am afraid that this phrase is thrown around so often that we easily lose sight of the personal and relational aspects of what it means to be a Christian. Instead, we reduce our walk with God down to a series of acts we know we are supposed to perform. Read the Bible. Pray. Go to church. Witness. Have a quiet time. Give to the poor. Do ministry. That's what it means to be a Christian. And make no mistake about it, each of these is important and good, and all should be a part of your life. Yet, if we are not careful, in the midst of all our activity for God, our connection to him can be lost. Instead of approaching him directly, we try to perform for him, as if he will let us be close to him only if we prove ourselves worthy. This path won't take us any closer to God. Instead, it leads only to frustration.

Owning your faith means more than filling your mind with Christian thoughts. It goes beyond standing on your own rather than relying upon your parents or youth pastor for the answers to the difficult situations in which you find yourself. And it also transcends living a life of purity and integrity that refuses to go along with the crowd. Owning your faith is embracing Christ and being embraced by him, not as a spiritual concept but as an act of desperation and love. It begins not with expending large amounts of time and energy trying to win God's favor, but with the realization that he loves you with a love our minds cannot fully comprehend.

THE LOVE OF GOD   First John 4:19 makes one of the simplest, yet most profound statements human ears have ever heard: "He loved us first." Long before we ever gave God a thought, back in the days when we just wanted to do our own thing and be left alone, God loved us. Not only that, he loves us at our worst, when we aren't exactly lovable.

Just in case we can't wrap our minds around this truth, God gives us a picture to help us figure it out. In the Old Testament, God told the prophet Hosea, a godly man with a strong walk with the Lord, to go down to the local red-light district and marry a street-walking prostitute named Gomer. Even though it went against all logic, Hosea did what God asked. After a few years of marriage, Gomer decided she'd had enough of the boring married life. She ran back to her favorite street corner and started selling her body again. She sank so deep into prostitution that she became a slave to her pimp. God then told Hosea to go back to the red-light district, buy her back, take her home, and love her as his wife. Once again, Hosea did exactly what God told him to do (see Hosea 1:2–3:3).

This is how God loves us. He is Hosea and we are Gomer. I know Richard Gere fell in love with Julia Roberts when she was a prostitute in *Pretty Woman*, but Hosea and Gomer's story is no Hollywood fantasy. God loves us when no one else will have us, and he loves us before we are respectable in his sight. Not only does he love us first, but like Hosea, he comes looking for us. He initiates the relationship we have with him. Our part of the bargain is to respond in faith, loving him as he loves us. Everything God requires of us in our relationship with him can be summarized in one command, "Love GOD, your God, with your whole heart: love him with all that's in you, love him with all you've got!" (Deuteronomy 6:5).

Even this act of loving God back comes from him. When you respond to him in faith, he plants his Spirit inside of you. You don't just learn about God from a distance. You experience him up close (see Jeremiah 31:33-34). He makes sure of it. Romans

8:15-16 puts it this way: "This resurrection life you received from God is not a timid, grave-tending life. It's adventurously expectant, greeting God with a childlike 'What's next, Papa?' God's Spirit touches our spirits and confirms who we really are. We know who he is, and we know who we are: Father and children." This is what it means to know God. This is the shortest distance between him and you.

MOVING BEYOND THE ROMANCE   Our love relationship with God resembles the other love relationships we experience in this life, at least from our perspective. Human love relationships go through many different stages. First there's the eye-catching phase, where you begin to realize that you sort of like that guy or girl and you wouldn't mind going out with him or her. Then there's the blooming romance stage, where you find this other person fills your every waking thought. As romance blooms, it grows into true love, a stage where you'll give anything and everything for the sake of your beloved. This is love at its most intense emotional level. But it often gives way to the "we're in a relationship" phase, where slowly but surely your true self comes out. All of this eventually leads to the "is this really the person I fell in love with?" phase. In this last stage, all those quirky little character traits you thought were so cute in the eye-catching phase and so endearing during the romance stage are now just plain old annoying. If you can't get past this stage, it often leads to the final phase of many relationships, the break up.

Even couples who have been married for decades have gone through most of these, including the "is this really the person I fell in love with?" phase. Relationships that last are those in which the couple chooses to love no matter what phase they may be passing through in that moment.

It should not surprise us, then, to learn that a relationship with God also passes through several stages. From a purely human standpoint, how we feel about God goes through emotional ups and downs. Our feelings change. The initial excitement of the new birth dies down as we grow accustomed to being saved. Some days we just don't feel very joyful or faithful. There are even days when we get mad at God. Or at least I do. The prophet Jeremiah did as well. If you're interested, read what he said to God in the heat of his anger in Jeremiah 20.

Yet none of our emotional ups and downs change the way God feels about us. He never gets so infatuated with us that he fails to see us for who we truly are. He's seen us at our worst, and he loves us anyway. Nor is he ever blinded by love. He never offers a standard, "But you don't really know them," when someone points out our faults. He knows our faults. He sees our inconsistencies, but that doesn't change anything. His love never wavers. It is the one constant through every phase we pass through in our love for him.

Which brings us back to where we started. God has opened a direct path for us that leads right into his presence. The whole point of this Christian life, the whole reason for embracing a faith that is truly your own, begins and ends here. God loves you and he wants you to love him back. Responding to him in kind is the beginning of what this faith is really all about.

AND ON THURSDAY NIGHT EVERYONE GOT SAVED (AGAIN)

CHAPTER 3

HERE'S THE PART THAT was the hardest for me to deal with. I can remember the day it started as if it were yesterday. I was in the middle of a quiet time, and I was praying in a closet in my apartment in Dallas, Texas. Yeah, I actually used a walk-in closet as my place to meet with God. I guess that came from growing up hearing the King James version of Matthew 6:6 over and over, "But thou, when thou prayest, enter into thy closet." (To get the full impact of the King James version of this verse, you really need to read it with your best Elizabethan actor accent.) So I entered my closet and I started prayesting, but something was different. My technique was no different from the day before or the day before that or the day before that, but I felt something I'd never felt before in my times alone with God.

I felt nothing.

No emotional lift.

No feelings of the presence of the Lord.

No warmth and reassurance that God heard my prayers.

Nothing. Zero. Zilch. Nada.

I didn't feel anything at all.

At first I tried praying harder. Most days I used the A-C-T-S acrostic as a prayer guide: Adoration, Confession, Thanksgiving, and Supplication (which means asking God for stuff). So when I didn't feel God's presence in my prayer closet like I had every other day, I poured all of my energy into the Adoration part of prayer. I praised God for who he is, and I listed off his character qualities that leave me in awe. With all of my spiritual might, I focused on the greatness and goodness of God. And still I felt nothing. After a few minutes, I finally stopped, opened my eyes, and said to the clothes hanging in the closet, "Hmmm, this doesn't seem to be working today. It's probably just me. I will try it again tomorrow."

But the next day wasn't different. And neither was the next day. Or the next. Or the next. As days turned into weeks and weeks into months, I got more than a little scared and confused. It wasn't just prayer. I didn't feel anything from God at any other time either. When I went to church, nothing. Sang praise songs, nothing. Read the Bible, nothing. I was in college studying to be a pastor at the time, and I didn't feel anything in my classes. That summer my wife and I served as counselors with our home church at camp. The week was amazing. God gave me the privilege of leading ten guys from my home church to Christ.

And I felt nothing.

Don't get me wrong. During the week of church camp I felt all sorts of emotions. I felt great joy over these guys who had a new-found relationship with God. I felt humbled and in awe that God would let me be a part of what he had planned for their lives. By the end of the week, I felt really, really tired, which is what you are supposed to feel by the end of church camp, even when you are there as a twenty-something-year-old counselor.

But I didn't feel that spiritual buzz. I didn't sense that closeness to God that I craved. I mean, come on, it was church camp. Everyone feels a spiritual buzz at church camp, especially on Thursday night when everyone gets saved. At least that's how it was when I was growing up. I went to a camp at a place called Falls Creek in the hills of southern Oklahoma. On Monday five thousand students would arrive with one thing on their mind: meeting members of the opposite sex from some other church. The girls from other churches always looked better than the ones from our church, even when they didn't. But by Thursday night, nearly every one of the five thousand students would either get saved or rededicate his or her life to God. And we would all feel it. That buzz. That high. That feeling unlike anything in the entire world. I always thought it had to be the kind of feeling that Moses felt when he was on top of the mountain getting the Ten Commandments from God. Man, what a rush. I loved that spiritual high.

After high school I ran away from God for a couple of years, but that ended in an even better feeling. The night I finally waved the white flag to God and told him he'd won, I felt a weight rising off of my shoulders. In that moment I experienced a closeness with God unlike anything I'd ever experienced before. This closeness went beyond the church camp high, because it didn't wear off. The only way I can describe it is that this was a feeling of God's presence. I knew he was with me.

Now it was gone, and nothing I tried brought it back. I prayed harder. I read my Bible like a crazy man. I went forward during the invitations at my church. I prayed with friends. I confessed every sin I'd ever committed, no matter how small. I even wondered if I ever really knew God at all. But nothing I tried removed the void I felt.

Finally, God showed back up, but only for a moment, and

only to deliver this simple message: It's impossible to please God apart from faith (see Hebrews 11:6).

SILENCE FROM HEAVEN   I wanted to share my story to let you know that, in all likelihood, you will have a similar experience. A day may come, if it hasn't already, when you will not feel God's presence. You will not feel that spiritual buzz during worship. You will not experience an emotional lift as you pour out your heart in prayer. Your relationship with God will feel like running into an old boyfriend or girlfriend on the street long after the last of the feelings you had toward them have died. All you will feel is nothing.

Then what?

I know, I know. This won't happen to you. My experience is an anomaly. God would never cut you off or leave you feeling abandoned. After all, Jesus said he would be with us until the very end of the world (see Matthew 28:20). God promised he would never leave or forsake us (see Hebrews 13:5-6). Romans 8:16 tells us that the Holy Spirit speaks to us deep in our hearts and reassures us that we are God's children. How could God make good on all these promises and we not feel it?

I don't know the answer to that last question, except to say that he does and at times we won't. That's what happened to Job. If you aren't familiar with Job's story, you should go read the first few chapters of the Bible book that bears his name. In one day, Job, one of the wealthiest guys around, lost everything, including his ten children. Not long afterward, he was struck with a terrible illness that left him covered with oozing boils from head to toe. He looked so bad, his closest friends didn't even recognize him. But that wasn't all Job lost. The first few verses of his book tell us that not only did he love and serve God, Job was identified as the best of the best by the Lord himself. No one had a walk with God like Job.

Yet when Job needed God the most, when his entire world had fallen apart and he had no one else to lean on, God wasn't there. At least it didn't feel like he was there from Job's perspective. He continually cried out in prayer, yet all he heard in return was silence. In the midst of his emotional agony, Job cried out,

> I travel East looking for him — I find no one;
> > then West, but not a trace;
> I go North, but he's hidden his tracks;
> > then South, but not even a glimpse. (Job 23:8-9)

I felt a very small snippet of the desperation Job expressed. I cried out to God, telling him I needed him, and he didn't do anything to let me know he'd heard me. Job didn't expect to hear a voice booming down from heaven. None of us do. But we at least expect God to let us know that he is there. In that moment we want to hear from him more than anything else.

AN INCONVENIENT TRUTH   Now here's the part where you start to think I've lost my mind. Fair enough. But keep reading.

The day in my closet when God suddenly became silent was one of the best days of my Christian life. In fact, if I was ever going to grow up spiritually, if I was ever going to mature in Christ to the point where God could actually use me to do anything of lasting significance, I needed God to pull back and leave me hanging. And you do too. I know that sounds exactly backwards, but it is true. The only way your faith will become your own is if God takes you to a place where you have nothing but faith to pull you through. No feelings. No emotions. No tangible reassurances that God is near. Nothing but faith. The experience is a lot like love. You may feel in love with someone, and you may feel like you cannot survive another day without them, but you haven't really experienced love until you know that you can survive without them but you choose not to. Love can't mature until the hormones and emotions die down, and faith cannot mature until everything that props it up is removed.

All of this comes down to the nature of faith. Hebrews 11:1 defines faith as "the certainty that what we hope for is waiting for us, even though we cannot see it up ahead" (TLB). Faith has absolutely nothing to do with emotion. It is not a feeling you have in the depths of your soul that what you hope for is somehow waiting for you up ahead. Instead, we are certain because we believe what God says. We know what we hope for is waiting for us because God promised that it would be there. Many times we don't have anything to go on except for the certainty that God has spoken.

In the book of Genesis, God told a guy named Abram that he would make him into a great nation, even though Abram and his wife were both pushing ninety and were childless. God even told the guy to go outside and try to count the stars. Then he said to him, "Your descendants will be like that—too many to count!" (Genesis 15:5, NLT). On a purely human level, God's statement doesn't make any sense. How many eighty-year-olds have you ever seen picking out baby clothes for their newborns? But Abram didn't look at things on a human level. Instead, he "believed the LORD, and the LORD declared him righteous because of his faith" (Genesis 15:6, NLT). Though Abram didn't see God's promise come true for another decade and a half, he never stopped believing.

This is faith on its most basic level. God speaks and we

believe, even without any tangible proof that we are on the right track. With nothing to go on except God's promises, we believe. That's faith. And you cannot please God without it.

Now here's the kicker of this whole shebang—at least it was for me. In the beginning of my walk with Christ, I needed those wonderful feelings, the tangible experiences that assured me God was nearby. They confirmed my decision to turn my life over to God with nothing held back. Those feelings were great back then, and to be honest, I admit that I still want them today. But, in the early days of my walk with God, if I felt some emotional or spiritual reply from him, or could sense his voice whispering through the noise of my daily life, I did not have to exercise faith. But when God cut me off from all emotional experience, when he left me with nothing to go on except a handful of promises in the Bible, I faced a choice. In that moment I had to decide how much I really believed this stuff. I had to ask myself if I believed it enough to stick with it even when it didn't feel like it was working.

This is a biblical dilemma God throws our way. In John 6, Jesus performed two mind-blowing miracles. First, he fed over five thousand people with five barley loaves and two fish that one of his disciples scrounged from a kid in the crowd (see John 6:8-11). Then, after sending the five thousand people home, Jesus went for a stroll across the Sea of Galilee during a storm (see 6:16-21). Only his disciples witnessed the latter miracle. Needless to say, Jesus had their attention. The next day, Jesus confronted a huge multitude with a message that didn't exactly endear him to the people. He talked about how he was the Bread from heaven that gives eternal life, and how people had to eat his flesh and drink his blood if they were to receive eternal life. By the time he finished, people in the crowd were murmuring, "This is tough teaching, too tough to swallow" (6:60), and many left, never to return. Instead of chasing after his dwindling crowd, Jesus turned to the Twelve and said, "Do you also want to leave?" (6:67).

In a sense, I heard God say these very words to me during the days of silence that stretched on for longer than I ever imagined possible. I had to examine my heart and figure out why I believed. Was it because believing made me feel better about myself and the world around me, or was it because Jesus is the embodiment of truth? Then I had to wrestle with whether I would still believe if this whole Christianity thing didn't feel like it was working for me. Eventually, you will need to wrestle with the same questions yourself.

Making your faith your own doesn't just mean figuring out what you believe and why you believe it. Nor is it simply taking a stand for Christ when everyone else goes another direction. Your faith becomes your own when, in the silence, you can say with Peter, "Master, to whom would we go? You have the words of real life, eternal life" (John 6:68). Not only does this make your faith your own, but it also opens the door for you to know God with a depth you cannot experience any other way. You will find an intimacy in the silence, and his presence made real even as you wonder if he is there.

MEET WITH ME

CHAPTER 4

ONE DAY IN A worship service, while we were singing songs about wanting to know God more and meeting him face to face, my mind started to drift, as my mind is prone to do. As we stood singing "I want to know you, . . . I want to see your face,"[1] I wondered to myself what would happen if God suddenly showed up and we were all granted our wish. Here we were singing about how we wanted to look deep into the face of our King, but I wondered: What would happen if he did the very thing we asked him to do? What would happen if God showed up in the middle of this worship service? Would the guy on the acoustic guitar keep playing? Would the drummer keep drumming and the worship leader keep singing? Forget them. What would I do if God showed up and invaded my space?

Psalm 22:3 says that God is enthroned on the praises of his people. This means that the act of heartfelt worship draws us into God's presence. When Christians worship, God is already there through his Spirit, who dwells inside every believer. Yet there are times he makes his presence known in unmistakable ways. In Acts 4:31 we can read how God caused a building to shake with the power of the Holy Spirit in response to the prayers and praise of a small group of believers. Later in Acts, God did the same thing to a prison as Paul and Silas sang praise songs while locked in a cell (see 16:25-26). So this makes me wonder: What would happen if God suddenly showed up in the midst of a worship service today?

GREETED WITH FEAR   My friend Corey gave me his answer. One Sunday morning he was standing in church, singing along with everyone else, doing his best to follow along with the words in the hymnal, when it happened. He told me an overwhelming sense of the Spirit of God came over him. "I felt like I could reach out and touch God right there with my hand," Corey told me, "and it scared me to death." This was a turning point for my friend, but not in a good way. As God pulled him close, Corey came face to face with God's desire for his life. He knew what he had to do. Like the rich young ruler, Corey heard God tell him to leave everything behind and go full bore after him. But Corey couldn't do it. God came near, and my friend pulled back. Corey hasn't come face to face with God's presence since that day, and he rarely goes to church anymore.

As strange as it may sound, Corey's reaction is not uncommon. When God showed up in the Old Testament, people almost always shrank back in fear. Sadly, like Corey, they often ran away. That's what the children of Israel did while camped at the base of Mount Sinai. Not long after God set them free from Egypt, Moses led them to the very mountain where the Lord had appeared to him in the burning bush. Once they arrived, Moses wasn't the only one to see God's pyrotechnics. A cloud descended onto the top of the mountain, which then began to shake as fire and smoke billowed like a furnace. A ram's horn sounded long and loud, even though no one was actually blowing a ram's horn. Finally, God's voice boomed from the mountain and the people heard it. Exodus records, "All the people, experiencing the thunder and lightning, the trumpet blast and the smoking mountain, were afraid—they pulled back and stood at a distance. They said to Moses, 'You speak to us and we'll listen, but don't have God speak to us or we'll die'" (20:18-19). Less than a month and a half later, Moses came down off the mountain to find these people who had pledged to serve the Lord worshiping a golden cow instead.

This whole episode strikes me as incredibly odd. I've never been so lucky as to get to see God shake a mountain and set it on fire. I've never heard his voice boom out of the clouds like thunder, and I don't know anyone who has. I don't know about you, but I think actually hearing God speak would get my attention. How could the Israelites be so dense as to worship a piece of lawn art as a god after such a close encounter with the real thing? But then I think of my friend. He doesn't worship golden cows, but he doesn't do much Lord worshiping anymore either. Why?

I think the answer to this question lies in another Old Testament story where God showed up in an unmistakable way. A prophet named Isaiah found himself in the midst of God's throne room. Two angels flew overhead singing God's praises with such loud voices that heaven's temple shook. God's glory filled the room like smoke, and through it Isaiah could see the Lord sitting on his throne. Immediately the prophet cried out with a Hebrew word that is translated several different ways in English Bibles. The word is more a sound than a word, a guttural combination of grief, fear, and dread. It's the kind of sound people make when they fall to their knees with the knowledge that their worst fears have been realized. Isaiah let out this sound because the moment he found himself in God's presence, he became acutely aware of his utter sinfulness, especially his sins of speech. He cried out,

> Doom! It's Doomsday!
>   I'm as good as dead!
> Every word I've ever spoken is tainted—
>   blasphemous even!
> And the people I live with talk the same way,
>   using words that corrupt and desecrate.
> And here I've looked God in the face!
> The King! GOD-of-the-Angel-Armies! (Isaiah 6:5)

Yet coming face to face with both God and his sin didn't cause Isaiah to pull back. Instead he experienced the cleansing power of God's forgiveness, and his life was never the same. He went on to become one of the greatest prophets in all the Old Testament.

Isaiah felt the same fear the people at Mount Sinai experienced. He experienced the sense of unworthiness that washed over my friend Corey when God showed up during a worship service. But the fear and unworthiness caused Isaiah to confess his sin and draw closer to God, not run away.

Isaiah's story turned out differently because his heart was different. And that's what God showing up exposes. His presence pulls back all the facades we hide behind and reveals the true nature of our hearts. The light of his face makes it impossible for us to lie to ourselves any longer. We have to come clean or run away. The experience isn't pleasant. In fact, it is downright painful. Yet it can be liberating if we respond to the invitation God makes as he speaks to us there.

CAN WE GET BACK TO SOMETHING A LITTLE MORE PLEASANT? Not all of these thoughts ran through my head as I stood singing in the worship service where this question first bounced around my brain. If they had, I probably would have tried to shove them out of my head and move on to something more pleasant. Wouldn't you? I don't write all of this to make you think that getting close to God will leave you worse off than when you started. It can, but only if you choose to harden your heart rather than lay it bare before God.

No, I write all of this as a wake-up call to some of us, and as a reminder to others of us, that knowing God—truly knowing him—is not an experience to take lightly. Worship occupies such a central place in the Christian life, that, if we are not careful, we can adopt a very casual attitude toward God. Even worse, we can get so caught up in the songs and the emotions of the moment that we lose sight of the One we are worshiping. When that happens, all of our songs and praise become nothing but noise.

At the beginning of the chapter, I wondered what would happen if God showed up during one of my times of worship. I have the equation backward. The truth of the matter is this: God has showed up. He's already here. The more I become aware of his presence, the more I understand his holiness, as Isaiah did, the more I will worship. I won't need to be prompted by someone else. I won't even need any music.

FINDING GOD One of the first truths we learn when we are little kids is that God is everywhere. As the psalmist declared to the Lord,

If I climb to the sky, you're there!
    If I go underground, you're there!

If I flew on morning's wings
    to the far western horizon,
You'd find me in a minute—
    you're already there waiting! (Psalm 139:8-10)

However, there is a difference between knowing God is everywhere and being aware of his presence in a deep and personal way. I knew a guy who used to keep in his office an empty chair, in which no one was allowed to sit. He told everyone that it was Jesus' chair. No one else could sit in it because Jesus was already there. Yet even this falls short of sensing the presence of God in a way that is as real and tangible as the way the children of Israel experienced him at Mount Sinai. This takes something more than an empty chair. It takes silence.

Psalm 46:10 presents one of the hardest challenges for those of us who live in the modern world: "Be silent, and know that I am God!" (NLT). The command "be silent" can also be translated "be still." The Hebrew word literally means to let ourselves drop like hay sinking down into a fire. *The Message* uses the phrase "step out of the traffic" for the word, which helps capture the sense of dropping everything, of removing ourselves from all the noise and distractions, so that our minds can sense the One we miss in the midst of the noise.

Most of our lives are filled with noise. From the music blaring from speakers or coming through our earbuds, to the television, to the constant flow of communication through phone calls, text messages, instant messages, and e-mails, an incessant stream of noise runs through our souls. Psalm 46:10 tells us to unplug, to silence ourselves and the noise around us, to step out of the traffic so we might know that God is God.

The second half of that command is the real kicker. It doesn't say to be silent so you can hear God, as if he has some special message he wants to deliver. Instead, God tells us to be still and simply know that he is God. Think about that for a moment. God wants us to step outside the barrage of mental traffic and allow the presence of the one true God to sweep over us. He calls us to sit and be quiet before him, for he has shown up. He is here, and he doesn't have to say a thing for us to know it. "Be still, and know that I am God," he tells us. Notice, the verse doesn't tell us what to do after that. It doesn't have to. We will know.

All of this brings us back to where we began. When God shows up, one of two things will happen. We will either run away in fear, or we will worship him from our innermost being. Either way, the light of his presence reveals the true nature of our hearts and our faith. The next test moves from our hearts to our minds and challenges us to do something few people want to do: think.

GOING DEEPER   Because of the brevity of this book, we can only scratch the surface in each of the four areas that lead to taking ownership of your faith. To dive deeper into what it means to know God intimately, consider reading the following:

- Jonathan Edwards, *The Religious Affections*
- Thomas à Kempis, *The Imitation of Christ*
- Francis Schaeffer, *True Spirituality*
- Charles Colson, *Loving God*
- Max Lucado, *He Chose the Nails*
- Charlie Starr, *Honest to God*

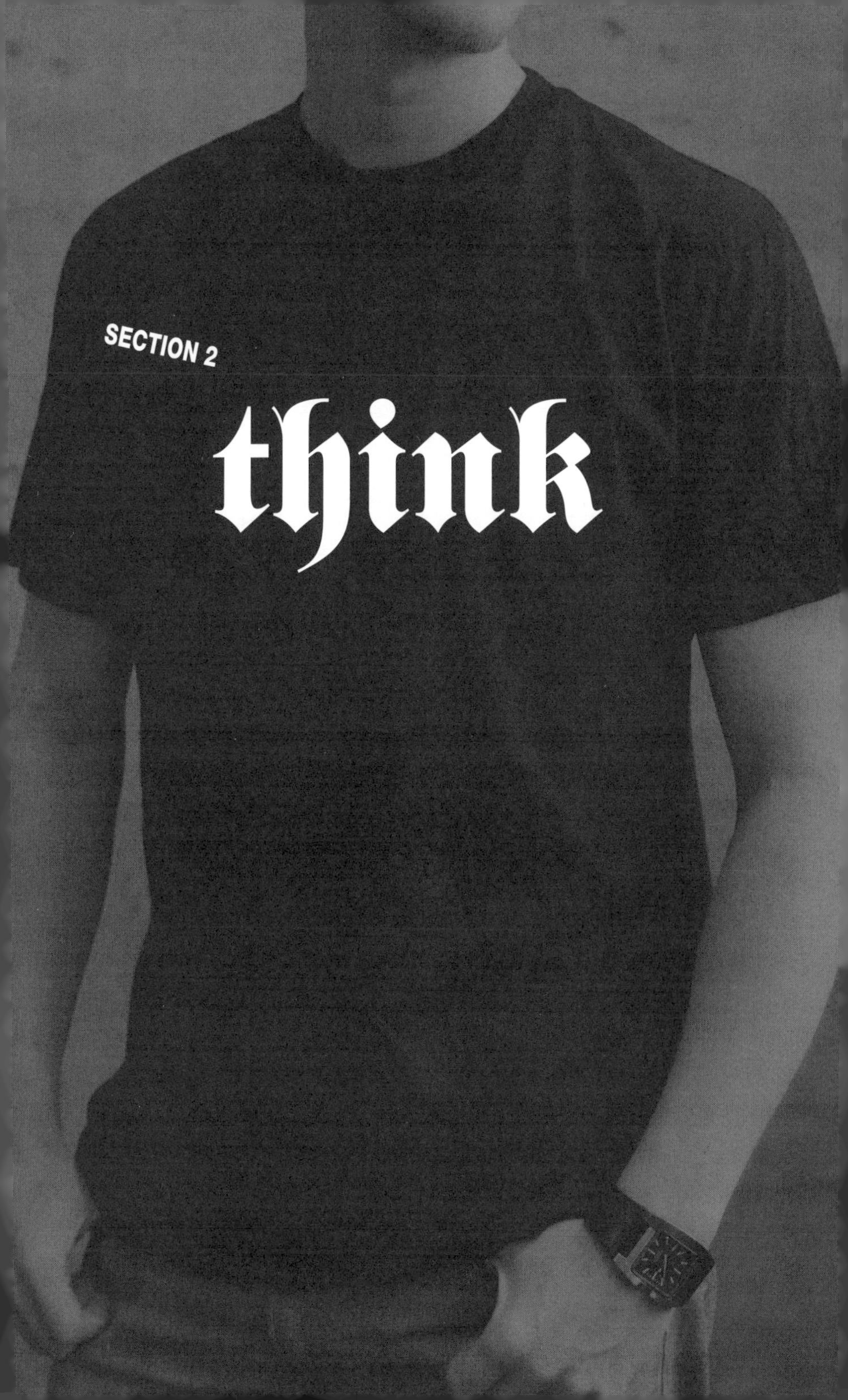
SECTION 2
think

QUESTION EVERYTHING

CHAPTER 5

THE TITLE OF THIS chapter isn't exactly what you might expect in a book like this. I'm supposed to help you grow in your relationship with Jesus, and here I am telling you to question everything. And everything means everything: Every idea you believe is true and every one you're sure is false—question them all. Pull out your beliefs about God, Jesus, the Bible, your ideas about the meaning of life, and even your beliefs about the way people showed up on this planet. Pull them all out of the recesses of your mind and ask, "Am I sure about this one?"

The fact is, you will question them all whether I tell you to or not. The title of this chapter is less a command than a statement of fact. Most people, when they get out on their own for the first time, go through a time of questioning everything they've ever thought and believed. It's normal. If I tell you not to do it, all I will do is waste the ink on this page and make you feel guilty without cause.

You need to question everything. In fact, asking questions needs to become a constant in your life from this point forward as you learn to think critically. Not many people take this step. You will encounter far more who simply soak up whatever is thrown their way without giving it a thought. I see this just about every time someone comes to my house for the first time. Near the front door hangs a photograph of the entire Tabb family atop a killer whale as it leaps out of the water in front of an enthralled crowd at Africa Marine World, USA in Vallejo, California. All five of us are yelling with our hands high in the air. You can see water streaming off the killer whale, although we somehow managed to stay dry. This picture has hung in our living room for over fifteen years, and for fifteen years people have asked the same thing when they see it for the first time: "Wow! Is that *real*?" We always tell them it is, and the people are truly amazed that we rode a killer whale like some sort of real-life Mountain Dew commercial.

The people who assume my wife and I took our three daughters for a ride on an orca are not gullible, unintelligent people who can barely feed themselves. Far from it. They are fooled because *Homo sapiens* as a species have a habit of accepting the reality presented to us. We all do it.

THE LAZY WAY   That's why you need to constantly think through every piece of information thrown your way. I recommend you start now, as you read this book. If you do, you will notice the contradiction at the beginning of this chapter. I told you that most people go through a period of questioning everything they've ever been told was true, and then, in the next paragraph, I claimed not many people are in the habit of questioning everything. How can both of these statements be true? It may seem impossible, yet they are.

Most people go through a stage of questioning everything they were told as a child, especially the things their parents told them. I did, and I didn't wait until I got to college to start. About the time I turned thirteen or fourteen, I thought my parents didn't have a clue about much of anything. At times I wondered how they could feed themselves. I know my own children have wondered the same thing about me. A quote attributed to Mark Twain sums up what most of us feel: "When I was a boy of fourteen, my father was so ignorant I could hardly stand to have the old man around. But when I got to be twenty-one, I was astonished at how much he had learned in seven years."[2]

Doubting the usefulness of everything your parents ever told you doesn't take much effort, nor does it lead to making your faith your own. In fact, it does just the opposite by playing right into the oldest trap the Devil ever used against the human race. When Satan tempted the first man and woman in the Garden, he started off by causing them to doubt the words of their parent, God. The Devil told them, "Do I understand that God told you not to eat from any tree in the garden? . . . You won't die. God knows that the moment you eat from that tree, you'll see what's really going on. You'll be just like God, knowing everything, ranging all the way from good to evil" (Genesis 3:1,4-5). With doubt as his weapon, Satan convinced Adam and Eve that God was holding out on them, that a world of incredible experiences was waiting for them—a world God wanted to keep for himself. Of course they fell for it, because they didn't think. They never asked why they should trust a talking snake more than God. Instead, they swallowed the lies the snake was dishing out, and the results were disastrous.

Doubting God and every other authority figure has been a part of the human experience ever since, and the results have not improved. It comes naturally to us, as if the default position of the human heart is set on disbelief when it comes to authoritative voices. We do this pretty well on our own, yet when we hear a new chorus of voices telling us how wrong all the voices we once listened to are, we take doubt to a whole new level. These voices aren't necessarily unwitting pawns of the Devil out to do you harm. Yet harm is exactly what they do when they lead you to dismiss ideas and beliefs you once held without thinking through the replacements they offer.

Questioning everything doesn't mean dismissing out of hand beliefs we held dear. Nor does it mean rejecting any new ideas simply because they are new. Both extremes are wrong. Instead, we need to learn to think critically about every claim to truth that comes our way. We need to learn to ask the right questions.

LOOKING BEYOND THE OBVIOUS   Asking the right questions changed the course of Dean's life without his even realizing what was happening. In the summer before his sophomore year of high school, he sensed God calling him to devote his life to some sort of ministry. Without thought, Dean said yes. Two years later he changed his mind, thanks to the deadly combination of spiritual immaturity, a smart mouth, and a low tolerance for a couple of little old ladies in his church, who tried to keep him on the right track by constantly telling him, "That's a fine attitude for someone who's going to be a preacher." By the time he graduated, Dean had decided that he would do his thing and God could do his. Dean still believed God existed, but that was about as far as his faith commitment went. All he wanted was for God to leave him alone, and he would return the favor.

For the next couple of years, Dean felt like God took him up on his bargain. No lightning bolts flashed as his language and lifestyle changed to suit his more enlightened self. Instead, God did something so sneaky, so underhanded, that Dean couldn't escape him if he'd tried. God planted three little words in Dean's head that he could never get past. Every time he tried to settle into his new-found freedom, he found himself asking, *And then what?* At first these three little words only jumped out when he contemplated college majors and career choices. But in time they started cropping up with every choice he made. No matter how hard he tried to do otherwise, these three words forced him to look past the immediate moment and gaze down the road to where every decision would take him.

The question in his head haunted Dean like a phantom from a Stephen King novel. When he sat in a philosophy class and listened as the professor discussed whether or not he or anyone else were really there, Dean could hear the question: *If this is true, then what? If this life is nothing more than an illusion, what now?* Then the question followed him into sociology class as the professor explained how all the rules that govern societies are nothing more than arbitrary decisions those in power use to stay in power. When the professor said, "Even in a society of saints, there will be sinners" (which basically means ultimate standards of right and wrong do not exist), the question popped into Dean's head: *If that is true, then what? What does it ultimately mean if right and wrong don't really exist?*

And the question in his head wouldn't quiet down when class was over. It forced him to examine every part of his life in the same way. When it came to choosing a career, Dean wanted to find something that would enable him to make a lot of money and give him the freedom to do whatever he wanted to do. But the annoying question in his head made Dean go one step further and consider what the point of such a life would be. *So you make a lot of money*, ran his thoughts, *maybe buy a big house and a nice car. Then what? Is that all you really want out of life?* The questions' constant noise made settling on a major more than a little difficult.

The questions that God planted in Dean's head weren't there to make him miserable. Instead, they were God's way of forcing him to think critically about the world and his place in it. He forced Dean to look at the world from an eternal perspective, even when he didn't want to. Ecclesiastes 3:11 says, "[God] has planted eternity in the human heart, but even so, people cannot see the whole scope of God's work from beginning to end" (NLT). God may not cause the words "and then what" to pop into your head every time you must decide whether or not something is true, but he has other ways of making you think beyond this world of time. He wants you to look beyond the obvious rather than simply swallow every idea thrown your way.

This, then, is what I mean when I tell you to question everything. Ask critical questions and search for answers. Your goal is to discover truth that will enable you to make sense of this world and to live life to its fullest. As you wander around asking "and then what?" the following three questions may help you sort through this process.

1. Is this true?

This is the most obvious question of all, as well as the most difficult to answer. Everywhere we turn, we hear claims to truth that contradict one another. How can we discern which claims are accurate and which are the equivalent of the thirty-year-old rumor that atheists are pressuring the Federal Communications Commission to ban all Christian radio and television stations? Start by putting ideas to the test. Examine how they line up with the world you see around you. The book of Job gives you an excellent example of how to do this. After Job's world fell apart, three of his friends came to cheer him up. Once they saw the depths of his suffering, they changed their minds. Job's friends believed that God always causes good things to happen to good people and bad things to bad people. Therefore, in their minds, the best way to tell how God feels about a person is to examine the person's current state of prosperity and comfort. A series of natural disasters and violent attacks had robbed Job of everything he owned, killed his ten children, and covered his body with oozing sores. If ever a man had ticked off God, Job's friends felt he had to be it. Yet Job countered his friends' arguments by pointing out how people who thumb their noses at God often live pain-free, trouble-free lives. As for Job's character, God himself said that no one on earth compared to him. Job's friends' ideas were not true, because they didn't line up with the real world.

Comparing ideas to reality isn't always so easy to do. For truth to be true it must also stand up through both space and time. Therefore, we need to think historically as well as globally as we examine ideas thrown our way. Some ideas sound great in a prosperous place like the United States, but they fall apart when you drop them into the Sudan, where Christians suffer for their faith, and fellow human beings die of starvation. During the Middle Ages, people believed the earth was the center of the universe, not because they were unintelligent, but because they didn't have enough information in front of them. Don't repeat their mistake.

2. If this idea is true, what are the logical implications?

Ideas do not exist in a vacuum. Every claim to truth sets off a chain of consequences like dominoes falling against one another, which ultimately change lives. For that reason, before we accept something as true, we need always to ask what dominoes it will knock over in our lives. Try asking yourself, how will my perception of the universe change if the information in front of me is true, and how will my life be affected by it?

The people on the eastern seaboard of the United States experienced this one Halloween night many years ago, when Orson Wells and a team of actors did a live radio version of H. G. Wells's classic, *The War of the Worlds*. Television didn't yet exist, much less twenty-four-hour news channels like CNN. So those who missed the first few minutes of the broadcast had no way of knowing that they were not in fact listening to live news coverage of a full-scale attack from beings from outer space. Widespread panic broke out as people ran shouting into the streets. These people weren't nuts. They knew that if flying saucers were indeed attacking New Jersey, life as they knew it would never be the same.

Every idea has the same power. In fact, ideas are the single most powerful force on the planet. Therefore we need to ask, what will this idea unleash in my life and the world around me if it is true?

3. If this idea is true, how must my life change to live it out?

Jesus said, "If you stick with this, living out what I tell you, you are my disciples for sure. Then you will experience for yourselves the truth, and the truth will free you" (John 8:31-32). When you believe something to be true, it will alter the course of the rest of your life. That is why we must look ahead and ask ourselves where the ideas and information thrown our way will ultimately take us. We also need to ask ourselves whether or not we can live in the world they create.

Looking ahead in this way was the final proof that led me to embrace the biblical account of creation rather than the naturalist approach my college biology professor spent weeks explaining. I didn't just reject naturalism out of hand. Instead I explored its logical implications. The naturalist explanation for the existence of life, which removes God from the equation, ultimately means that all of creation is the result of a series of accidents and coincidences. If that is the case, then there is no higher purpose to life, no rhyme or reason to why things happen as they do. Nor are there any absolutes. Laws and regulations are nothing more than arbitrary rules someone with power imposed on those without power. Consequently, in the naturalist's universe, there is no inherent difference between helping a little old lady across the street and shoving her in front of a bus. Whatever laws there may be against the latter have no ultimate authority beyond the power of local government. I can't live in that kind of universe. No one can.

That's the purpose of this third question. Look ahead to where all the claims of truth you encounter will ultimately take you. Again, ideas are the single most powerful force in the world. They always have been. Ideas plot the course of history and determine the fate of all the world's inhabitants. Where are your ideas taking you?

~

As you begin asking these questions, you will soon discover that to find the ultimate answers you need something more than the chorus of voices surrounding you. To discern truth, you need a source of truth that can always be trusted. For the Christian, that source is an ancient book that many people talk about, but far fewer ever explore for themselves.

IMMERSED IN TRUTH

CHAPTER 6

IF WE WANT TO take possession of our faith and grow up spiritually, we have to read the Bible. I would like to find a better verb than "read" to explain what we need to do with God's book, but the English language doesn't leave me many options. I need something stronger, a word that means more than eyes moving across a page, but read is all I have. Perhaps I should say we need to devour the Bible or study the Bible or internalize the truths of the Bible, but those words don't say what I want to say, either. They imply that we need to dig deeper into each and every verse to uncover truths the casual reader never sees. There's a place for in-depth Bible study, but it isn't the key to making your faith your own. For that we must allow God's story, which is his Word, to sweep over us. Reading the Bible means losing yourself in its pages like you would with Michael Crichton's latest thriller. The reason for this is twofold, and both elements go to the heart of what God wants to do in your life.

BEYOND FINGERPAINTING At its most basic level, God's plan for our spiritual lives is for us to grow up in him. All of us start out in Christ as the spiritual equivalents of little babies. Most people find babies to be cute and cuddly and adorable, at least most females do. Yet, no matter how gaga someone goes over babies, most everyone except the parents and grandparents backs away when the child starts crying or spewing or emitting one of those strange odors babies are known to emit. That's just how babies are. They are cute, but also very high maintenance, and extremely vulnerable to harm. Newborns can't hold their over-sized heads up, and they also have a soft spot on their head that must be carefully guarded. As for basic human skills such as feeding and cleaning themselves, forget it.

Spiritually, that's how we start off in God's family. New Christians are fun and exciting and ooze an enthusiasm that you can't help but catch, but they also require constant care, attention, and protection. We don't expect little babies to do much more than eat, sleep, cry, and poop. That's part of the wonder of new life. However, we call it a tragedy when a child grows older, but never matures beyond the infant stage. The same holds true of our spiritual development. A Christian who never matures is just as much a tragedy. The writer of the book of Hebrews addressed just such a group of believers when he said,

By this time you ought to be teachers yourselves, yet here I find you need someone to sit down with you and go over the basics on God again, starting from square one—baby's milk, when you should have been on solid food long ago! Milk is for beginners, inexperienced in God's ways; solid food is for the mature, who have some practice in telling right from wrong.

So come on, let's leave the preschool fingerpainting

exercises on Christ and get on with the grand work of art. Grow up in Christ. (Hebrews 5:12–6:1)

The human body needs the right nutrition to grow, and the same holds true of our spirits. Feasting on God's Word is the only way to grow beyond spiritual fingerpainting exercises. As you read the Bible, you grow and mature in your relationship with God, as well as gain the spiritual strength you need as you set out to serve him. The Bible is key, because your spiritual life in Christ started through the Word. First Peter 1:23 tells us, "Your new life is not like your old life. Your old birth came from mortal sperm; your new birth comes from God's living Word. Just think: a life conceived by God himself!" After you are born again, the same Word that produced life in you now fuels your spiritual development in the same way food fuels the human body.

At this point I'd planned on inserting some long explanation of how reading the Bible causes you to grow, but to be quite honest, doing so wouldn't make you want to read the Bible any more than a long, scientific explanation of how the human body converts food into energy makes you want to eat. Hearing how I should eat something because it is good for me ends up making mealtime a chore rather than a joy, just as being told to read the Bible for its spiritual nutrition squeezes all the fun out of God's Word. When I take a bite of chicken parmesan, I don't think about how my body will process the protein of the chicken or the calcium in the mozzarella cheese or the sucrose in the tomato sauce. Instead, I relish every bite because I love chicken parmesan. Just writing about it is making me hungry.

The Bible works in the spirit just as food works in the body. The point isn't how it works, but the joy that comes as you savor every part of it. We shouldn't read God's Word because it is good for us, but because it is good. Too often we forget this crucial distinction. We approach the Bible like it is God's medicine cabinet and thumb through it in search of a spiritual vitamin that will make us feel better. Instead, we need to immerse ourselves in the story that is the Bible. True joy comes as you allow yourself to get lost in its pages and get caught up in the wonder of God at work. As we read we feel his heart and the gentle touch of the Spirit impresses himself on our spirits. That's how the Bible is to be read. That's how it seeps deep into our souls and allows us to grow up in Christ.

A PROPER PERSPECTIVE ON REALITY   The Bible not only fuels our spiritual growth, it also changes the way we see the world around us. As we read, the Word becomes the lens of truth through which we view all of reality, allowing us to see the world from God's perspective. Put another way, for the believer, the Bible serves as the baseline of understanding for all other areas of knowledge. This doesn't mean the Bible is the only place we ever need to turn to learn anything worth knowing. Obviously, there is no way to squeeze everything we need to know about everything into its sixty-six books. For example, the Bible covers the creation of the entire universe, including every plant and animal species, in only thirty-one verses. That's not exactly an exhaustive treatment of such an important subject. Yet it tells us the crucial truth we need to know: God made everything, and he made it with both order and wonder.

The Bible doesn't have to go into minute detail on every subject to affect our understanding of all knowledge. Genesis 1 may not give a detailed description of how the universe was created, but it serves as the baseline to our understanding of the sciences by telling us *who* created it. In the same way, the Bible changes the way we see other people—regardless of their race, gender, nationality, or social standing—by telling us that God made every human being in his image. It also helps us understand why people do the things they do by telling us how these wonderful creatures, made in God's image, rebelled against God and plunged the entire human race into the darkness known as sin.

As we read the Bible, God turns on the lights of our understanding and allows us to see reality through his eyes. This, too, is a crucial part of the work God wants to do in your life. He wants you to become mature in your relationship with him and in your understanding of truth. Paul put it this way in his letter to the Ephesians: "No prolonged infancies among us, please. We'll not tolerate babes in the woods, small children who are an easy mark for impostors. God wants us to grow up, to know the whole truth and tell it in love—like Christ in everything" (4:14-15). Knowing the whole truth doesn't just apply to matters of faith, but to all areas of knowledge. As we will see in the next chapter, all truth is ultimately God's truth.

You can take this from the realm of theory and make it a part of your life in a couple of ways. One approach says you make the Bible the baseline of your understanding on any given subject by studying every verse related to that subject. Do you want to understand the issues related to the sanctity of life? Look up everything the Bible says about life and how God created it. Do you want to understand the issues surrounding the poor and a Christian's responsibility toward them? Look up the word "poor" in a concordance or do a search for it in an online Bible index. According to this approach, all you need to do to gain God's perspective on any given subject is to search out a list of Scriptures related to that subject.

This approach has merit, and there are times when it is the

best way to gain a biblical perspective on a hot-button topic. However, this slice-and-dice approach to the Bible doesn't give you the full picture of what God wants you to know. It also strips most of the fun out of reading the Bible. I could take the same approach with one of my favorite Michael Crichton novels, *Jurassic Park*. Both the book and the movie make a very strong statement about scientific responsibility and the ethics of discovery. In one section, Crichton delivers a stinging indictment, "Scientists are actually preoccupied with accomplishment. So they are focused on whether they can do something. They never stop to ask if they *should* do something. They conveniently define such considerations as pointless. If they don't do it, someone else will."[3] I could quote other lines from the book and convince you that ethics and science cannot be separated, but wouldn't you rather read a story about genetically engineered dinosaurs running amok? I know I would. When I read the story, the larger point comes through so loudly that I can't miss it, as it is delivered through the context of the characters' unfolding struggle for survival.

The same is true of the Bible. God could have inspired its writers to write a textbook or an encyclopedia of everything we ever needed to know about the Lord, but were afraid to ask. He didn't use either approach. Instead, when we begin reading the Bible we quickly find ourselves immersed in a story that unfolds throughout all sixty-six books. God's storytelling didn't begin the day Jesus told his first parable. It is how he chose to deliver his eternal truth to us from the very beginning. From Genesis to Revelation, God's Word tells his story, and as we lose ourselves in it, his truth washes over us. As it does, we grow up spiritually; and our understanding of God, ourselves, and the world around us radically changes.

HOW TO READ   All of this brings us back to the point I've been trying to make since the opening lines of this chapter. Making your faith your own means having your heart and your mind transformed in such a way that you begin to think like Christ. God makes this possible by giving us his Spirit. According to 1 Corinthians 2:16, "we can understand these things, for we have the mind of Christ" (NLT). That doesn't mean that God drops all eternal knowledge into our heads all at once with no effort on our part. Rather, God gives us his Spirit, his mind, which then gives us the ability to understand his eternal truth. Those who do not know Christ do not have this privilege; but because we have Christ's Spirit living inside of us, his Word comes alive as we read it, and our lives are transformed.

That is why the single most important thing you can do is read the Bible. And by read I do not mean picking out a verse here or there. If you truly want to make your faith your own, if you truly want to stop relying on a parent or a pastor for your understanding of God, read the Bible in its entirety. Start at the beginning and read through to the end. Don't worry about uncovering a promise you can carry with you each day. Just read. You will quickly find the Bible is much messier than the sanitized Sunday school stories would lead you to believe. That's part of the beauty of reading God's story for yourself. Wrestle with the messy parts. Be enthralled by the glorious parts. Allow the wonder of God to leave you in awe. And don't be afraid to ask questions. It's okay to scratch your head at times and say, "I don't get it." You will find that people in the Bible did that very thing as they lived through the events you will read about.

I know from experience that starting in Genesis and reading through to Revelation can be a difficult task. I've found that reading the Old and New Testaments at the same time helps me understand both parts. Also, reading the Old Testament in the order in which the books appear in the Hebrew Bible helps me see God's story with greater clarity. I've included a reading schedule in the back of this book that combines both of these elements. Following it will take you through the Bible in one year. Another option is *The Message//Remix: Pause; A Daily Reading Bible* (Colorado Springs: NavPress, 2006), in which the Bible has already been arranged into 365 daily readings for you. If that's too slow for you, at the back of this book I've also included a reading schedule that will take you through the Bible in one month.

Whether you read the Bible in one year or one sitting, the important thing is to read it for yourself. Not only will reading be a vital part of the journey to make your faith your own, it also prepares you for the struggle of reconciling God's eternal truth with the ideas thrown your way every day in the classroom. With the Bible as your baseline of understanding, you are ready to think.

I HAD TO READ A BOOK BY STEPHEN HAWKING FOR A PHYSICS CLASS

CHAPTER 7

PEOPLE LIKE TO BUY books that make bold predictions. The old soothsayer Nostradamus, who allegedly foresaw everything from the rise of Adolph Hitler to the death of Princess Diana, has been dead for nearly four hundred and fifty years, yet he is more popular than ever. If it worked for him, it can work for me. So here goes, my bold predictions for the future. . . .

Prediction number one: A tornado will touch down somewhere in Oklahoma this year. It will probably hit a trailer park.

Prediction number two: A hurricane will move through the Gulf of Mexico at some time between June 1 and November 30. I also predict that the Home Depot closest to the predicted route of the storm will sell out of plywood.

Prediction number three: An earthquake will strike California. In fact, and I know I am really going out on a limb here, I predict that multiple earthquakes will strike California this year. They won't all be large, and some may not be felt, but they will hit. Speaking of earthquakes, I predict more than ten major earthquakes will strike various places in the world in the next twelve months.

Finally, prediction number four: I predict that beliefs and truths you've taken for granted will be called into question while you are in college. And I predict (I'm really on a roll now) that this will happen to you even if you go to a Christian college.

I must stop predicting now. I'm feeling a little light-headed after exerting so much psychic energy. Whew. Who knew pulling a Nostradamus could take so much out of you? Of course, unlike the long-dead prophet, I didn't speak in generalities. I made bold assertions that I guarantee will come true.

What's that you say? How can I predict the future with such certainty? You can call it a gift. Or, if you are of the more skeptical bent, you might point out that tornadoes hit Oklahoma every year, and the same goes for hurricanes in the Gulf of Mexico and earthquakes in California. Predicting at least ten major earthquakes in the world isn't much of a leap of faith, since the United States Geological Services records an average of nineteen major earthquakes across the globe each year. When you live in a place that experiences tornadoes or hurricanes or earthquakes every year, you shouldn't be surprised when one comes along. Instead, you should prepare yourself ahead of time so that, when the inevitable happens, you will be ready.

PREPARING FOR THE STORM   Proper preparation is the key to surviving the inevitable storms that will confront your faith. Rest assured, the storms will come. I went to school with a guy who nearly lost his faith while attending a Christian college that specialized in training pastors. Brian's faith hit a wall in a class on theology, which is more than a little ironic since theology means the study of God. Imagine nearly losing your faith while studying the object of your faith in a class and a college that believes every word of the Bible is completely true. Brian's problem arose from a couple of books he read for a paper he had to write. The books presented ideas that contradicted everything the guy had ever been taught about God, and they did it with an eloquence and logic that blew him away. By the time he finished the paper, Brian found himself in full crisis mode as he was forced to think through ideas he'd never before considered.

Brian had thought he was prepared for the questions he would encounter while researching that paper. He knew the answers to skeptics' questions, but having a handful of prepackaged responses wasn't enough, not when the skeptics had even better responses to his proofs. Brian had been taught what to think, but he'd never learned *how* to think, and, as a result, he nearly lost his faith.

The difference between being told what to think and learning how to think is the difference between a faith that is your own and one that is nothing more than an extension of those who programmed your mind. How can you tell which you have? You've already experienced the difference in your relationship with every math student's best friend, Bob, aka, Mr. Back of the Book. When brains lock up and an answer is nowhere to be found, Bob comes to the rescue . . . as long as the problem has an odd number. Bob may not know much about even-numbered problems, but Bob has never met an odd-numbered problem he couldn't solve.

Writing down the answers from the back of your math book is being told what to think. Understanding the hows and whys behind the answers and being able to use those steps to answer the even-numbered problems requires knowing how to think. Bob can help you learn how to think by reassuring you that you are on the right track as you check your work on the odd-numbered problems. However, when all you know is what Bob tells you, you are in trouble.

You need more than the spiritual equivalent of Bob to help you through the tough questions you face. I know, I know, you've faced tough questions in science classes since you were in grade school. The picture in your science book showing the progressive evolutionary generations from ape to human isn't exactly an affirmation of the first three chapters of Genesis. Yet having a backpack filled with prepackaged answers to hard questions is not enough. That is not to say that books that address the hard questions serve no purpose. Far from it. However, these books are like Bob. Understanding how they arrived at their answers is just as important as the answers themselves.

What, then, do you need to do to think for yourself and find the answers to the questions on your own?

STEP ONE: BUILD ON THE BASELINE   Proverbs 9:10 says, "For the reverence and fear of God are basic to all wisdom. Knowing God results in every other kind of understanding" (TLB). Solomon, the author of Proverbs, had more than religious understanding in mind when he penned these words. He contends that anyone who wants to understand the true nature of any part of the created universe must begin with the God who made it. The eternal Creator, who exists outside of the limitations of the physical universe, is the starting point for every other realm of knowledge, especially the sciences.

This conviction drove many of the founders of modern science, including Newton, Pasteur, Faraday, Bacon, and Pascal. Francis Schaeffer maintained that:

> the majority of those who founded modern science, from
> Copernicus to Maxwell, were functioning on a Christian

base. Many of them were personally Christians, but even those who were not, were living within the thought forms brought forth by Christianity, especially the belief that God as the Creator and Lawgiver has implanted laws in his creation which man can discover.[4]

As part of my preparation for writing this chapter, I interviewed two research scientists who both said their work is built on the conviction that God both created and controls all of creation. Both base their work on the laws that God established in the natural order. One told me, "What God has created is a wonderfully complex system that could not have been designed any other way except by an intelligent Creator."

Since the day the Catholic Church came out against both Copernicus and Galileo and their idea that the earth revolved around the sun, science and theology have often been at odds. The division arose in spite of the fact that Copernicus dedicated his *De Revolutionibus Orbium Coelestium* (*On the Revolutions of the Heavenly Spheres*, 1543) to Pope Paul III, and both Copernicus and Galileo thought of themselves as good Catholics. The rift grew wider in 1859 when Charles Darwin published *The Origin of Species*. For many, the separation became complete in the summer of 1925 when John Scopes went on trial for teaching evolution in Dayton, Tennessee. Today the relationship between science and the Bible is so poisoned that many people see them as mutually exclusive.

They don't have to be. The Bible begins with the simple statement, "In the beginning God created the heavens and the earth" (Genesis 1:1, NLT). John echoes Genesis when he declares, "He created everything there is. Nothing exists that he didn't make"

(John 1:3, NLT). If these statements are true, and Christianity is built upon the conviction that they are, then we can expect to find God's fingerprints all over his handiwork. And we do. Our God is a god of order and beauty, and both shine out in the natural world. Not only that, but since the God who created all things is the God who has revealed his true self through the Bible, we should also expect to find consistency between the way God describes his creation in his Word and what we find as we explore the physical universe. Simply put, with God as our starting point, we will find that science and the Bible complement, not contradict, one another.

STEP TWO: KEEP AN OPEN MIND   Reconciling science and the Bible is not an either-or proposition, although many try to make it so. Those who do fall into two camps. The first group sees apparent contradictions between science and theology and relegates the Bible to the realm of myth and legend. Today, less than 30 percent of Americans believe the Bible is the actual Word of God and should be taken literally.[5] The other 70 percent do not reject the Bible completely; however, many compartmentalize the Bible and Christianity into the spiritual realm and view them as completely separate from the real world. Most believe in a God who can make life better and more fulfilling, but they look to science, not God for explanations of the origins and development of life.

Others go to the opposite extreme, rejecting any and every scientific theory out of hand as antithetical to the Bible. A few years ago, a Christian major league baseball player caused a stir when he declared that dinosaurs never existed, based on the fact that they are not mentioned in the Bible. How could he say such a thing in the face of the largest, most complete, and best preserved *Tyrannosaurus rex* fossil yet discovered, which is permanently displayed in a museum not far from where he played baseball? To him, the fossils didn't matter, because they are used to validate a theory that is not confirmed by the Bible. All that matters is the Word of God, and since it doesn't mention dinosaurs, the case is closed.

Extreme positions in either direction cause us to miss out on the wonder God has revealed in both his Word and his world. Ecclesiastes 7:18 says, "It's best to stay in touch with both sides of an issue. A person who fears God deals responsibly with all of reality, not just a piece of it." Solomon's words are especially relevant here. God has made himself known to the world in a general way through his creation, and in a specific way through his Word. Keeping an open mind means looking for the places where God's two realms of revelation overlap one another. For the believer, God is our baseline of understanding; he is the Master Artist who spoke everything into existence. Now our job is to unleash the curiosity he planted inside of us to discover how he crafted his universe.

STEP THREE: KNOW YOUR LIMITATIONS   Not only did God give his Law to Moses, he also penned the laws of physics that make life possible in our universe. However, our ability to understand both God's Word and the physical universe is limited by our finite nature. If that weren't bad enough, our perceptions are also skewed by our sin. In Romans 1:19 Paul wrote that God placed his truth inside the human heart and scrawled it across his creation. However, our sinful natures cause us to push that truth aside. Paul went on to explain, "What happened was this: People knew God perfectly well, but when they didn't treat him like God, refusing to worship him, they trivialized themselves into silliness and confusion so that there was neither sense nor direction left in their lives. They pretended to know it all, but were illiterate regarding life" (Romans 1:21-22).

This means that even though all truth is God's truth, we can't always understand it. God declared through the prophet Isaiah:

"I don't think the way you think.
    The way you work isn't the way I work."
        GOD's Decree.
"For as the sky soars high above earth,
    so the way I work surpasses the way you work,
and the way I think is beyond the way you think."
(Isaiah 55:8-9)

For millennia philosophers and scientists have tried to unlock the secrets of the universe; yet the more they discover, the more, they realize, they do not know. On any scale you can devise to measure it, the universe God created is far more complex and wonderful than our minds can imagine, and this limitation skews our understanding of truth.

These shortcomings play out in what we think we know about God and the world around us. Facts may be observed correctly, yet that doesn't guarantee that the inferences drawn from those facts will also be correct. That is why a sense of apprehension hung over the world as January 1, 2000 drew closer. Some experts feared that a programming shortcut would cause every computer on earth to shut down at the stroke of midnight, with the onset of the new millennium. Beginning with the earliest computers, to save space programmers used two digits for dates rather than four. Experts predicted that this flaw would make computers think the year 2000 was in fact 1900, and all programming would freeze up as a result. Some Y2K Bug prophets of doom predicted airplanes would fall from the sky, banks would fail, and the world as we knew it would end. In case you haven't heard, none of the doomsday predictions came true. The experts had their facts straight, but the conclusions they drew from them were wrong.

Why are experts so often wrong? Because we as human beings are limited by our finite nature and the sin that infects us all. As God says in 1 Corinthians 1:19, "I'll turn conventional wisdom on its head, I'll expose so-called experts as crackpots." You must keep this in mind as you sort through the barrage of information thrown your way. We human beings like to claim we know far more than we actually do. Yet history is littered with discarded theories that everyone once "knew" were facts. Understanding the human limitations of knowledge and understanding can keep your faith from getting swept away.

STEP FOUR: SEARCH FOR TRUTH   When it comes to discerning truth, there is no room for laziness. Too many students are so used to being spoon-fed what they are supposed to believe, that when they go off to college they swallow anything. Instead, we need to read, research, and listen. Our baseline of understanding comes through reading the Bible, but our reading shouldn't stop there. As we find ourselves confronted with differing ideas and theories, we need to read from different perspectives and listen to other voices, then put these ideas through the filter that God's perspective provides. Again, the goal is finding truth, not landing on some theory that makes the most compelling case.

That's how this chapter got its name. A couple of months prior to starting on this book, I picked up a book by Stephen Hawking called *The Universe in a Nutshell*, which explores string theory, black holes, and the space-time continuum, all in an attempt to discover the essential nature of the universe and a unified theory of everything. The book itself is short with lots and lots of illustrations. I have to read it in small bites, because thinking through the warping of time and Heisenberg's Uncertainty Equation makes my brain hurt. So why would I voluntarily choose to read a book like this? I'm not a masochist. I'm curious. I want to keep learning, to keep searching for all of God's truth wherever it may be found.

GOING DEEPER   To explore the ideas of this section in greater detail, consider reading the following:

On critical thinking:

- G. K. Chesterton, *Heretics*—an enjoyable read that feels like it was written yesterday, not 100 years ago. It is available for free as an e-book at ccel.org.
- C. S. Lewis, *Mere Christianity* and *The Abolition of Man*—the former is a must. The latter shows how absolutely necessary critical thinking truly is.
- Allan Bloom, *The Closing of the American Mind*—this is not a Christian book, nor is it an easy read. However, Bloom's insights are worth the effort.
- J. P. Moreland and Mark Matlock, *Smart Faith*—explores what it means to love God with your mind, identifying fallacies in your beliefs and others'.

On the Bible:

- The Navigators, *The Bible: Think for Yourself About What's Inside*—a reader's guide to the Bible.
- The Navigators, *Theology: Think for Yourself About What You Believe*—this book not only explores the faith, it makes you think through all you believe without spoon-feeding you answers.
- Paul House, *Old Testament Survey*—don't let the boring title fool you. This book opened my eyes to a whole new understanding of God's story as it unfolds in the Old Testament.
- God, *Holy Bible*—there's nothing quite like going straight to the source.

On science and God:

- Francis Collins, *The Language of God: A Scientist Presents Evidence for Belief*
- Hugh Ross, *The Creator and the Cosmos: How the Latest Scientific Discoveries of the Century Reveal God*
- Lee Strobel, *The Case for a Creator*
- Stephen Hawking, *The Universe in a Nutshell* and *A Brief History of Time*

SECTION 3

Serve

THE FINE PRINT

CHAPTER 8

THE FEDERAL TRADE COMMISSION requires all advertisements to adhere to a strict set of truth-in-advertising rules. These rules require that all ads be truthful and non-deceptive; the advertisers must have evidence to back up their claims, and advertisements cannot be unfair. Advertisers didn't worry too much about truth in the first half of the twentieth century. Back then professional athletes like Joe DiMaggio and Arnold Palmer appeared in cigarette ads and promoted the health benefits of smoking. Julep cigarettes went so far as to claim that chain-smoking their brand would leave your breath pleasant and inviting.[6] But today, thanks to truth-in-advertising rules, weight loss commercials come complete with small print at the bottom of the screen that says "results not typical," and ads for prescription drugs always end with statements like, "May cause hair loss, drowsiness, dry mouth, and spontaneous bursts of English accent."

This chapter is the truth-in-advertising disclaimer for the following chapters in this section, both of which explore ministry. I didn't want to include it, because I thought it might scare some of you away. But rules are rules, and write it I must. My office assistants, who double as my legal counsel, told me I had to tell you what you are getting yourself into if you take all this talk of serving Christ by serving others seriously. I tried to tell them that in all likelihood you've already sampled some sort of ministry, such as a mission trip with the youth group from your church, but they wouldn't hear of it. Mission trips and other short-term ministry projects tell you about as much about real ministry as a ten minute test drive tells you about a used car. You think you know what you are getting yourself into, but . . .

That's where this chapter comes in. Most of us enter into the world of ministry with a set of romantic ideals floating around in our heads. We can hardly avoid it. Books abound that tell us how God has a unique and wonderful purpose for our lives. And he does. God designed each one of us with specific talents and skills that will enable us to fulfill his plan for our lives. He shaped our personalities, gave us special abilities and a singular outlook on life, and even bestowed supernatural spiritual gifts upon us, all "so that we can do the good things he planned for us long ago" (Ephesians 2:10, NLT). I don't know about you, but the thought of embarking on the grand adventure God has planned for me makes me feel a little like Moses on the day he walked down the mountain after seeing the burning bush. Ministry sounds like it will be the stuff of Hollywood—Indiana Jones meets Billy Graham.

That's how it sounded to me before I dove into it. Twenty-something years later, my view is a little more—how shall I put this?—subdued. God has given me some grand adventures, like the day I shared Christ with inmates on death row in Texas. But I've also learned that the grand adventure days are, in truth-in-advertising terms, not typical of the day-to-day business of ministry. If they were, sticking with the work of being a servant for

Christ would be easy. It isn't. Becoming a servant will provide a constant source of testing for your faith. Each and every day you have to make decisions that show how much you really believe all this talk of God and Jesus. More than that, you will also have your confidence in God pushed to its limits.

That's what happened to me, but, as the fine print says, *Your results may vary. Consult your ministry professional before beginning any vigorous ministry regimen. Understand that as you embark upon a lifestyle of serving God through serving others you risk the following:*

Truth-in-advertising disclaimer #1: You may experience extreme discomfort due to the counter-cultural nature of Christian ministry.

Ministry goes beyond good works. It's about more than feeding the hungry or visiting lonely, forgotten people in nursing homes. The heart of ministry comes down to meeting the single greatest need of every person on planet Earth: the need to be reconciled to God. The Bible says that all of us have committed acts of sin that separate us from a holy God. Romans 3:10-18 shows how seriously flawed we really are:

> There's nobody living right, not even one,
> nobody who knows the score, nobody alert for God.
> They've all taken the wrong turn;
> they've all wandered down blind alleys.
> No one's living right;
> I can't find a single one.
> Their throats are gaping graves,
> their tongues slick as mud slides.

Every word they speak is tinged with poison.
They open their mouths and pollute the air.
They race for the honor of sinner-of-the-year,
litter the land with heartbreak and ruin,
Don't know the first thing about living with others.
They never give God the time of day.

The only solution for this universal human condition, the only way we can have our sins forgiven and be set right with God is Jesus Christ. Acts 4:12 boldly declares, "Salvation comes no other way; no other name has been or will be given to us by which we can be saved, only this one." John is even more blunt: "This is the testimony in essence: God gave us eternal life; the life is in his Son. So, whoever has the Son, has life; whoever rejects the Son, rejects life" (1 John 5:11-12). This same message runs throughout the Bible. Since the beginning of time, the Lord God has placed an exclusive claim on the souls of people. He declares in Isaiah 43:10-11: "I alone am God. There is no other God; there never has been and never will be. I am the LORD, and there is no other Savior" (NLT).

Our calling, as followers of Jesus, is to plead with those who have not experienced the life God wants to give them through his Son, and offer them the gift of God's forgiveness. Paul wrote to the Corinthians, "We are Christ's ambassadors, and God is using us to speak to you. We urge you, as though Christ himself were here pleading with you, 'Be reconciled to God!' For God made Christ, who never sinned, to be the offering for our sin, so that we could be made right with God through Christ" (2 Corinthians 5:20-21, NLT). Every other act of kindness and mercy builds upon this central task. If it doesn't, we might as well do nothing at all. What good does it do to feed a starving child and prolong her life on this earth if we do nothing to help her experience the eternal life that will satisfy the hunger of her soul?

The truth that salvation can be found in Jesus Christ alone isn't just for the hard-core, godless pagans out there. This message also applies to Muslims, Buddhists, Hindus, Mormons, and everyone else who worships any god other than the God of the Bible. It also calls out to Jews, who call on the God of the Old Testament but reject Jesus' claim to be the Messiah. Christianity isn't a "live and let live" approach to life that says we can choose whether or not to feed the hungry or clothe the poor or even that all gods are the same regardless of what we may call them. Therein lies the risk. The exclusive claims of Christ fly in the face of a culture that values tolerance and acceptance above all. When you take Jesus seriously and share his good news as the only way to God, you open yourself to ridicule.

Immediately before he ascended into heaven, Jesus told his disciples,

> "God authorized and commanded me to commission you: Go out and train everyone you meet, far and near, in this way of life, marking them by baptism in the three-fold name: Father, Son, and Holy Spirit. Then instruct them in the practice of all I have commanded you. I'll be with you as you do this, day after day after day, right up to the end of the age." (Matthew 28:18-20)

Taking his instructions seriously enough to risk alienating others in the hope that they will listen and be reconciled to God places us at risk of rejection and extreme discomfort. But that's not the only risk we take.

Truth-in-advertising disclaimer #2: Doing the work of ministry may result in performing obscure and boring tasks that no one ever notices.

A couple of years ago, I was introduced to one of the most exciting (in terms of heart-pounding thrills) ministries I've ever witnessed. Stephen Baldwin's *Livin It* skate tour brings together some of greatest extreme sports athletes and puts on a show unlike anything you have ever seen. I'm old enough to remember when skateboards had metal wheels and in just riding one down the sidewalk one risked personal injury. I never thought I would see anything like the tricks these guys from King of Kings Skateboard Ministry pulled off. Then, when Chaos on Wheels, an extreme BMX team took over, I went from impressed to overwhelmed. At the end of the extreme sport exhibition, Stephen Baldwin shared his testimony, followed by a pastor who explained how anyone can have a relationship with God through Jesus. My favorite moment was watching Stephen and his wife stand in the hot August sun with their arms wrapped around little skater dudes, praying with them as they received Christ. The *Livin It* team repeats this scene over twenty weekends every summer and fall.

In 2005, this little skate and BMX bicycle show helped over five thousand people make commitments to Christ. Boring and obscure are the last words one would ever use to describe this ministry; X Games meets Billy Graham with a little *Bio-Dome* thrown in on the side is more like it. However, this ministry functions only because of the nameless and faceless volunteers who set up the portable skate parks in parking lots and empty fields, string wire, and set up the electronic equipment that allows the message to be heard. They also serve food to the athletes, transport them to the airports and hotels, and support the entire operation with prayer. No one ever gives a standing ovation to the guy on the sound board, yet, according to Stephen Baldwin himself, unless the people in the shadows do their jobs, *Livin It* would grind to a halt.

God assigns to very few people the job of serving others in the spotlight. To the rest of us he gives tasks that very few people will notice and fewer still will appreciate. Now here's the counter-intuitive part of this whole equation. Jesus told us to seek the shadow roles, not the big, visible positions everyone notices. He told his disciples, "So you want first place? Then take the last place. Be the servant of all" (Mark 9:35). As servants of Christ, we are to choose the small places, the last-place positions, until God shoves us into greater prominence.

The idea of nobly choosing to serve in small places may spark some romantic ideal inside you. Don't let it. Small means small, and small often means mundane and unappreciated. Or worse.

Melanie and Chêz had a lot of free time during their senior year at a Christian university and decided they could best fill it with a ministry that would bring glory to God. So they volunteered at a government-sponsored program for parents called Parents Anonymous. They took care of the children while the parents took the classes. However, most of the families in the program came from at-risk situations. The parents were either foster parents, who had to take the classes to stay certified, or moms and dads who'd been ordered to attend by the family court.

On the first night, Melanie and Chêz quickly discovered that their "ministry" wouldn't at all be what they had expected. The two college seniors were to watch three infants, six toddlers, one handicapped child who was ten, and four other children between the ages of five and twelve. The kids had Melanie and Chêz outnumbered, and they knew it. Instead of creatively sharing God's love with the children, Melanie and Chêz engaged in crowd control. To make matters worse, most of the children came from situations that left them filthy and sick. The last night of the program was the icing on the cake. While no one was watching him, one seven-year-old snuck into a corner and pooped on the floor. The rest of the children managed to step in the pile of poop and track it everywhere. Melanie and Chêz's adventure in ministry ended with them on their hands and knees, armed with wet paper towels and Febreze, trying to scrub the poop out of the carpet.

The real test of our faith comes not when we are asked to face death for the sake of God's kingdom, but when we are asked to clean up poop for those who neither recognize nor appreciate what we've done. God doesn't really care if we are willing to go out and change the world. He's looking for those who are willing to venture into the church nursery and change diapers. In God's eyes, there are no small tasks or big tasks, no small places or big places; there is only obedience. He notices something as small as offering a cup of water in Jesus' name. Even so, there aren't a lot of people clamoring to become God's water boy.

Truth-in-advertising disclaimer #3: Your ministry efforts and your life may not turn out the way you expect.

If you want to know what to expect when you devote your life to fulfilling Christ's call to follow him as a servant, read the stories of others who heeded his call before you. The Old Testament prophets would be a good place to start. Jeremiah is my personal favorite. Here is a guy whom God called when he was a little kid, a man in whom God implanted his words with fire. Jeremiah devoted his entire life to calling the nation of Judah back to God. How did the people respond? They didn't. Of course, Jeremiah's results may not be typical.

This whole ministry proposition can be more than a little frustrating. Some of God's servants experience incredible results, while others toil away and never see much of anything happen. That's why God compares his work to farming. I've never been a farmer. I have enough trouble getting grass to grow in my backyard, let alone trying to coax food-bearing plants to come up out of the ground. But I do know this about farming: It involves a lot of work that isn't always visible. Long before farmers can harvest a crop, they have to plant seeds in the ground. To the uninitiated, a freshly planted field looks like nothing more than acre upon acre of dirt. That's how ministry often appears. We may spend more time planting and watering than we do actually watching our efforts bear fruit. Looking out at a field of dirt, it's easy to feel like you are wasting your time, especially when the field right next to yours has plants popping up everywhere.

But that's not the worst of it. I hesitate to keep writing, because I want you to walk away from this section energized and ready to go out and change the world for Jesus. Maybe you will. Maybe yours will be the generation that sees lives change on a scale previous generations never imagined possible. However, you also need to realize that your life on earth may turn out like Jesus'. In the next chapter, we will journey deeper into the world of ministry, beginning with a look at the story of Jesus healing a man with congenital blindness. As that story unfolds in John 9, it reveals a further risk inherent in ministry—even the ministry of Christ himself. The incredible miracle did not cause huge crowds to flock to Jesus asking what they needed to be saved.

Instead, because Jesus healed the man on the Sabbath, this miracle enraged the spiritual leaders of the day. They argued with the blind man, threw him out of their synagogue, and started hatching plots against Jesus.

You may experience the same kind of resistance from the very people to whom you try to show God's love. Not only do they not always accept that love, they will, at times, turn against you. When it happens, you will find it much easier to walk away than to keep trying to reach out to hard-hearted people who could care less about God. If you find yourself in that position, you will be in good company. Isaiah, Jeremiah, David, Job, and Paul all shared your experience. Like them, you will have to decide how much you really believe all this stuff you say you believe.

Ministry involves risks. Lots of risks. You know your faith has taken hold of your soul when you understand the risks and go forward anyway. In that moment, it is truly your own.

MUDDY HANDS

CHAPTER 9

THE STORY WAS SO familiar to me that I'd never really noticed the weirdness of it until just the other day. Perhaps "strange" or "mysterious" would be holier descriptions, as in "the Lord works in strange and mysterious ways," but to me, the story is just plain weird. Jesus never did anything else quite like it.

The story goes like this: Jesus and his disciples pass a blind guy on the street, which prompts the disciples to launch into a debate over whether this guy brought his blindness on himself with his sin, or if his parents' sins did it to him. Apparently, at this point in time, Jesus' disciples subscribed to the theory that anything bad that ever happens to you in this life is God's way of paying you back for disappointing him. It's a very common theory. Jesus cut off their debate by saying, "You're asking the wrong question. You're looking for someone to blame. There is no such cause-effect here. Look instead for what God can do" (John 9:3).

So far the story is vintage Jesus. But then he does something that throws this episode into the realm of the weird. Jesus leans over and spits on the ground. He rubs the spit into the dirt until it turns into mud. He then takes the spit-mud he just made and pastes it on the guy's eyes. As he does, he tells the guy to go and wash in the Pool of Siloam, a man-made pool near the Temple in Jerusalem. The Greek word translated "wash" implies that the guy was supposed to do more than wash the mud off his eyes. Jesus told him to put his whole body in the pool, not just his face. As the mud washes off the man's eyes, he sees for the first time in his life.

I can't help but wonder what it was about this particular blind guy that made Jesus deviate from his normal *modus operandi*. Usually, when he decided to do a miracle, he simply spoke and BAM! Instant miracle. He didn't even have to be in the same zip code as the people he affected. His words were enough to make anything happen anywhere. When it came to healing the blind, Jesus occasionally touched their eyes to restore their sight, and one or two other times he applied spit to their eyes. Yet in this one instance he felt compelled to make some mud out of spit and rub it on a blind man's eyes like a healing salve. I don't know if you've ever made mud out of spit, but I have. I haven't done it since I was about seven years old, but I remember it left me with dirty hands and drove mud up under my fingernails. By the time Jesus finished this miracle, the blind man wasn't the only one who needed to find a place to hose off. Needless to say, I doubt if anyone was eager to shake Jesus' hand until he found a pool himself.

This story leaves me with an image I can't get out of my mind. The Son of God, the One who spoke the galaxies into existence, stands in front of me with dirty hands. A man with congenital blindness walks away with 20-20 vision while the One responsible for the miracle is left picking mud from under his fingernails. I don't mean to overanalyze the story, nor do I want to make the mistake of reading more into it than I should, but I can't help but hear Jesus ask me to get my hands dirty as he stands in front of me. He came to serve, not to be served, and that is my calling and yours as well. When Jesus served, lives changed. His acts of service opened the eyes of the blind, made the lame walk, and raised the dead. He went so far as to say that his followers would do even greater things than he accomplished. But, and this is a very important *but*, doing these "greater things" will leave us with dirty hands both figuratively and literally.

THE MARK OF A DISCIPLE Taking hold of Jesus' muddy hand and joining him in serving others is the third step in making your faith your own. In fact, it ultimately is the test of whether or not your faith is real at all. Jesus said it himself when he told his disciples:

> "When he finally arrives, blazing in beauty and all his angels with him, the Son of Man will take his place on his glorious throne. Then all the nations will be arranged before him and he will sort the people out, much as a shepherd sorts out sheep and goats, putting sheep to his right and goats to his left.
> "Then the King will say to those on his right, 'Enter, you who are blessed by my Father! Take what's coming to you in this kingdom. It's been ready for you since the world's foundation. And here's why:
>
> I was hungry and you fed me,
> I was thirsty and you gave me a drink,
> I was homeless and you gave me a room,
> I was shivering and you gave me clothes,

I was sick and you stopped to visit,
I was in prison and you came to me.'

"Then those 'sheep' are going to say, 'Master, what are you talking about? When did we ever see you hungry and feed you, thirsty and give you a drink? And when did we ever see you sick or in prison and come to you?' Then the King will say, 'I'm telling the solemn truth: Whenever you did one of these things to someone overlooked or ignored, that was me—you did it to me.'" (Matthew 25:31-40)

Jesus went on to explain how the goats on his left will be condemned because they failed to do all the things the sheep did. The goats, Jesus said, will be just as surprised as the sheep. "Master, what are you talking about? When did we ever see you hungry or thirsty or homeless or shivering or sick or in prison and didn't help?" (Matthew 25:44). I can understand their surprise. Who wouldn't stop to help Jesus if he needed it? But the King will reply, "I'm telling the solemn truth: Whenever you failed to do one of these things to someone who was being overlooked or ignored, that was me—you failed to do it to me" (Matthew 25:45).

The sheep are then herded into heaven, while the goats are taken off to a place of eternal doom. The only difference between them is what they did or did not do. Jesus doesn't mean to imply salvation can somehow be won by doing good deeds. The Bible makes it plain that God accepts us by our faith alone. In Galatians 2:16, Paul wrote, "We know very well that we are not set right with God by rule-keeping but only through personal faith in Jesus Christ." Yet real faith will result in a heart that cannot ignore the needs of others. James put it this way,

> Does merely talking about faith indicate that a person really has it? For instance, you come upon an old friend dressed in rags and half-starved and say, "Good morning, friend! Be clothed in Christ! Be filled with the Holy Spirit!" and walk off without providing so much as a coat or a cup of soup—where does that get you? *Isn't it obvious that God-talk without God-acts is outrageous nonsense?* (2:14-17, emphasis added)

The difference between God-talk and God-acts is the difference between a faith that is real and self deception. Owning your faith not only means internalizing a set of beliefs, but also allowing those beliefs to so permeate your soul that the very definition of a normal lifestyle for you changes. Compassion for the poor and powerless is normal for Christ followers. Recognizing the needs of people whom others easily overlook is normal for Christ followers. Caring about society's throw-away people is normal for Christ followers. In brief, a lifestyle of serving others is normal for a believer. Yet we don't stir up acts within ourselves because we know we need to do them. The presence of the Spirit of Christ in your life changes the way you see people and compels you to act. That is the difference between being a sheep and being a goat. Sheep have muddy hands, but fail to see anything particularly commendable about that fact. Goats keep people at arm's length, lest the dirty lives of those in need rub off on them.

WHO SWITCHED THE PRICE TAGS? If you grew up in church, this chapter may sound like someone just switched the price tags on you. When you are young, everyone tries to make God fun for you. Going to church can feel like a live, interactive VeggieTales video. Most children's churches are jam-packed with puppets, videos, games, and songs complete with all sorts of wild motions. Then, when you graduate to the youth group, or the student ministry, or whatever your church calls their special program for junior high and high school students, the fun hits a higher note. You go to camps and retreats and lock-ins, all of which come with high doses of loud music, games, caffeinated carbonated beverages, and pizza . . . lots and lots of pizza. Then there's the annual pilgrimage to Kings Island or Six Flags or whatever large amusement park is near you. In between, you have regular student worship services (whatever it may be called in your church), which are also high energy, and highly entertaining. That's usually the common denominator for your church experience when you are between the ages of 0 and 18. God is fun and church is entertaining.

Now I'm telling you to go get your hands dirty serving dirty people. If it feels like a bait and switch, maybe it is. I realize many of you have been involved in dirty-hands mission projects while you were in high school. The youth pastor in my home church takes a group of students down to the poorest part of the Appalachians every summer. There they spend a week working on people's houses and sharing Christ. Our church also sends teams to Mexico and Brazil for hands-on missions experience. Other churches in our area have taken students down to the Gulf Coast to help with hurricane relief. Yet there is a key difference between a short-term mission project with an enthusiastic group and a lifetime of getting your hands dirty serving others.

Richard Foster once said, "Large tasks require great sacrifice for a moment, small things require constant sacrifice."[7] Mission trips call for the former, as you give up a couple of weeks of your summer, mixing some fun with hard work. A lifetime of dirty-hands ministry calls for the latter, as you take the initiative to serve others in ways that no one notices. I could tell you how good you will feel when you start serving others. Or I could use the old line about how when you give to others you receive a greater blessing than anything you can give away. I could say that, but I won't, because such talk misses the point. When we truly understand what Jesus is all about, when his love for us takes hold of our hearts and this faith becomes who we are, we will become a servant whether we receive any tangible benefits or not. We will serve because we can't do otherwise. Dirty-hands ministry is the natural result of living a life that has ceased to be about you.

This is Christianity at its most basic level. And no one I know embodies this idea quite like my friend Greg.

FROM THE CORE

CHAPTER 10

GREG HAS NEVER QUITE gotten used to being saved. The new of his new life has never worn off. More than anything else, he wakes up every day astounded that God would love him enough to give his only Son on his behalf. The thought of it leaves Greg with the biggest, cheesiest smile you've ever seen and with some good news he just has to share. And share it he does. Everywhere Greg goes, he tells people about Jesus. When I first got to know him, Greg would spend his Friday nights dragging a large wooden cross along the main strip in his hometown. The lines of cars filled with people with nothing better to do than drive up and down the same one mile stretch of road slowed as they passed, the people inside honking and laughing, but Greg didn't mind. When someone would stop long enough to ask him about the big cross on his shoulder, he would smile and tell them about the love that he could never get used to.

That's just the way Greg was and is. Theologians would say he has the gift of evangelism. They may be right, but his gift is not what drives him. God's love does that, and it moves him to do some pretty crazy things. Several years ago, Greg and I were in a grocery store together. While I wandered up and down aisles looking for the things on my list, Greg headed over to the beer section. I found him walking among the cases of Budweiser and Miller Lite, slipping gospel tracks into each one. When I asked him what he was doing, he just laughed and said, "Man, people think this stuff will make them feel better, but I'm giving them something that will *really* make them feel good."

Shortly after Greg and I got to know one another, a man in our church took him to northern Mexico to conduct a Vacation Bible School for children in a small village. Although Greg and his wife, Michelle, never had children of their own, the kids who streamed into the VBS captured their hearts. Greg went back a few months later. The following year he bought a large, portable movie screen and a sixteen millimeter projector, which he set up as an outdoor theater that showed the *JESUS* film night after night. The more time he spent in Mexico, the more he felt the needs of the people around him.

Now Greg and his wife spend most of their time south of the border, spreading Christ's love to anyone who will listen. They train local pastors, conduct dental clinics, and go into schools and prisons with the good news that Greg still hasn't gotten used to. And they still conduct Vacation Bible Schools. In 2006 they helped more than eighty churches with VBS and had more than twenty thousand children attend. Greg and Michelle's ministry has grown beyond Mexico to Africa and Asia. They support nearly forty native pastors and an army of evangelists who also use the *JESUS* film to share the good news. In 2006, the guy who wakes up smiling because Jesus loves him had a part in introducing one hundred and fifty thousand people to the God he loves. He never set out to do something this big. It all just sort of happened because the new of his new life never wore off, even after twenty years.

URGED ON BY HIS LOVE   I don't think Greg ever gives much thought to why he drags a cross down the street or puts tracts in cases of beer or invests his life in the poor of northern Mexico. For him, serving others flows out of the relationship he enjoys with his God. Greg has discovered the secret of ministry, of expressing love to God by reaching out to those made in God's image. He embodies 2 Corinthians 5:14-15, which says,

> Whatever we do, it is because Christ's love controls us. Since we believe that Christ died for everyone, we also believe that we have all died to the old life we used to live. He died for everyone so that those who receive his new life will no longer live to please themselves. Instead, they will live to please Christ, who died and was raised for them. (NLT)

Everyone who receives new life in Christ can no longer live a self-serving, self-indulgent lifestyle. That doesn't mean we are incapable of self-absorption or that putting others before ourselves comes naturally. However, when the Holy Spirit takes up residence inside of us, he reshapes our desires. When he controls our desires, we will live to please the One who died and was raised from the dead, rather than to please ourselves. He doesn't use guilt or obligation to motivate us. Pleasing Christ by serving others isn't the spiritual equivalent of typing out a twenty-five-page research project on the second Punic war. Far from it. In *The Message*, verse 14 above reads, "Christ's love has moved me to such extremes. His love has the first and last word in everything we do." Serving others, sharing the good news of Christ, doing what Christians call ministry, all result from experiencing God's love first-hand. When we understand both mentally and experientially that Jesus loves us more than our minds can ever comprehend, we will want to love him back by loving those who bear his image.

I cannot emphasize enough how important that last paragraph is in this entire discussion of ministry. There's no shortage of voices telling us that we need to do more for God. The voices are everywhere: Give to the poor! Tell people about Jesus! Volunteer to help in the church nursery! Serve meals to the homeless! Do this! Do that! The list never ends. After reading this chapter, some might think they need to build a seven foot wooden cross and drag it down the main street of their town for a while, then maybe jump on a plane and fly to some poor, remote region of the world to serve as a missionary. Just writing about these things makes my own guilt level rise, because I'm not doing "enough." When the chorus of voices telling us what we need to do fills our ears, it's hard not to feel guilty.

I don't want to add to the guilt burden, because ministry isn't about guilt. Yes, a faith that is real is a faith that serves. But doing acts of service because we know we have to or because we think God will be very disappointed in us if we don't, is not faith. With God, *why* we act is just as important as what we do. He doesn't keep score to see who is doing the most. Nor is he necessarily the most pleased with those whose acts of selflessness are most impressive on a human scale. He never says, "Wow, get a load of Jim down there. He just donated a kidney to some guy he doesn't even know!" God looks through what we do and peers directly into our hearts. In Jeremiah 17:10 God says,

"But I, GOD, search the heart
　　and examine the mind.
I get to the heart of the human.
　　I get to the root of things.
I treat them as they really are,
　　not as they pretend to be."

The poor need to be fed and the oppressed need someone to rally their cause. As far as they're concerned, if you act on their behalf for the wrong reasons, it is still better than no one doing anything at all. However, on a personal level, acts of service must flow out of a heart of love and gratitude toward God. If not, we might as well do nothing at all. Paul put it this way, "If I give everything I own to the poor and even go to the stake to be burned as a martyr, but I don't love, I've gotten nowhere. So, no matter what I say, what I believe, and what I do, I'm bankrupt without love" (1 Corinthians 13:3). This love isn't some fuzzy feeling that sweeps over us, but a response of our hearts to the heart of God. It is the ultimate expression of faith. Paul wrote to the Galatians, "For in Christ, neither our most conscientious religion nor disregard of religion amounts to anything. What matters is something far more interior: faith expressed in love" (5:6).

This defines real ministry. Acts of love flow from the core of who you now are in Christ and express both faith and gratitude toward your God. It's not about what you have to do or should do or ought to do if you really mean business with God. It's all about who you are as a beloved child of the almighty Father. He loves you. Ministry means letting his love overflow from your life into the lives of others.

IMAGO DEI　Ministry not only flows from the core of your relationship with Christ, it also taps into the core of God's design for your life. You carry within you the *imago Dei*, the very image of God. This not only means that you were created with the capacity to know God, but that God made you like himself. At no point in our lives are we more like God than when we do what he does. Since Jesus came to serve, not to be served, we are most like him when we do the same. Therefore, in a very real sense, we unleash God's image in our lives by devoting ourselves to love and good deeds. The image of God in us reaches its fullest potential as we give our lives in service to others. The results can be very exciting.

God can be described in many ways. He is holy. He is love. He is compassionate and merciful. He is just. And he is creative. Very creative. Because he made us in his image, he made us with a creative spark. In the words of writer Paul Johnson, "We are, by our nature, creators as well. All of us can, and most of us do, create in one way or another. We are undoubtedly at our happiest when creating, however humbly and inconspicuously."[8] Since God's image in us reaches its fullest potential when we serve him by serving others, it stands to reason that the divine creativity he planted in us when he designed us will also be unleashed through acts of ministry.

In the book of Exodus, when God wanted his people to build a place where he would meet with them on a regular basis, he gave craftsmen the skills and artistry to build a place of worship worthy of the one true God. He told Moses,

> "See what I've done; I've personally chosen Bezalel son of Uri, son of Hur of the tribe of Judah. I've filled him with the Spirit of God, giving him skill and know-how

and expertise in every kind of craft to create designs and work in gold, silver, and bronze; to cut and set gemstones; to carve wood—he's an all-around craftsman." (Exodus 31:2-5)

Bezalel and the other craftsmen weren't building a place for themselves, but for God; and as they did, they created like they never had before. By doing so they imitated God who filled the universe with indescribable beauty, not for his benefit, but for ours.

All of this means that ministry that flows from the core of who God made you to be involves letting your creative juices run wild. As we do this, we will find that everything we do becomes a way of serving God by serving others. From the arts to something as mundane as mowing a yard, everything we do we are to do for God's glory (see 1 Corinthians 10:31). When God is glorified, lives will be touched and people will be changed. The only limitation is your imagination. This is what it means to serve without grudge or obligation. When you serve from the core of your being, the work of ministry doesn't feel like work at all.

NOW WHAT?   All of the above sounds great, but there's still one question hanging over your head: Where do you start? How do you find *the* task God wants you to do? How can you discover that place that will combine your unique gifts with God's calling? Many, many books have been written to try to help answer that question, and with all due respect to far more talented and insightful writers than myself, I don't believe you have to go looking for the specific ministry God has in store for you. Newton's first law of motion says that bodies in motion tend to stay in motion and bodies at rest tend to stay at rest unless an outside force acts upon them. Newton may as well have been talking about ministry. Many people sit around doing nothing, waiting for the hand of God to push them into action. However, I've found that it is much easier to feel God directing you toward the tasks he has in store for you if you put yourself in motion, actively looking for ways to serve him by serving others and taking the initiative to act wherever you may be needed.

The first thing I ever really did for God, aside from all the youth group stuff that I did more for fun than for the Lord, was install some toilets in my home church. I heard the pastor say something about needing to buy three or four toilets to finish out the bathrooms in a new addition in the church. Since I worked in a plumbing supply warehouse and could buy toilets wholesale, I volunteered. After helping to install toilets, I ended up on top of a ladder changing light bulbs. Soon my one night of building maintenance turned into a regular habit of helping out around the church wherever I could. That ministry put me on a path that led to a couple of career changes and eventually to the decision to use the gift of writing as a full-time ministry. I didn't even like to read back when I was installing the toilets in the upstairs church bathroom. I never would have guessed where this journey would take me.

In my experience, God reveals his plan to those who are already actively serving him. That's where you need to start. Look around. What do you see that needs to be done? Begin with your local church. Where can you help? Look around your neighborhood or your campus. What opportunities do you see to show the love of Christ to others? Experiment. You never know how God has gifted you to serve until you try. Begin with several different short-term ministry tasks. Then broaden your scope and volunteer for short-term missions projects, both in the United States and abroad.

My friend Greg didn't set out to be a missionary. Never in his wildest dreams did he imagine that one day he would help start churches and train pastors on three different continents. He was just a guy who worked on the assembly line at General Motors by day, and dragged a cross up and down the main strip of Midwest City, Oklahoma by night. As he allowed the love of Christ to flow from his life, God took over and put him right where he needed to be. Greg is far from unique. Who knows what God may have in store for you?

GOING DEEPER   I've found that nothing gives insights into what it means to serve God like reading the stories of those who gave their all to serve him. The first few books fall into this category. The rest explore the hows and whats and whys of ministry:

- Howard and Geraldine Taylor, *Hudson Taylor's Spiritual Secret*—an absolute must read. Available free of charge as an e-book at ccel.org.
- Courtney Anderson, *To the Golden Shore: the Life of Adoniram Judson*—one of the most moving books I've ever read.
- Elisabeth Elliot, *Through Gates of Splendor*
- J. R. Briggs, *When God Says Jump*—explores the lives of some biblical folks who took big risks for God.
- Richard Foster, *Celebration of Discipline*
- Marjorie Thompson, *Soul Feast*
- Rick Warren, *The Purpose-Driven Life*
- Francis Schaeffer, *No Little People*

SECTION 4

connect

THE OBVIOUS CHAPTER

MAKING YOUR FAITH YOUR own doesn't mean going it alone. You can try, but the odds are against you. A lifestyle of flying solo as a Christian usually guarantees disaster, for God never intended for us to live that way. At the beginning of time, when the earth's population was one, God declared, "It's not good for the Man to be alone" (Genesis 2:18). He then rectified the situation by doubling the population to two. The first man needed more than a mate to ensure the survival of the race. He needed another person with whom he could relate on an intimate level, someone with whom he could share his life. Each of us feels the same need, because God designed the human animal with an intrinsic need to connect with other people in a meaningful way. Every time we feel this need, we reflect the relational nature of the triune God.

So I guess that fact makes this chapter seem rather superfluous. I might as well include a chapter on how your body needs food, water, and oxygen. There may be a handful of hermits out there who could move off to a remote cabin in Montana and never see another person again as long as they live, but most of us enjoy having friends, even if our circle of friends is very small. To be completely honest, there's a bit of potential hermit in me. My wife says I'm almost there, since I spend hours at a time all alone in a little room, pecking away at a keyboard. But even I, near-hermit that I am, feel the need to connect. I cannot wait for the silence of my house to be broken by the noise of my wife and daughters coming home from work and school.

I need people. You need people. All God's children need to connect with people. Amen. Hallelujah. Now that that's settled I can end this chapter and move on to tell you something you don't already know.

THE OBVIOUS PROBLEM But, of course, I can't end this obvious chapter because, when it comes to relationships, we as a species have some work to do. God created us to connect with one another in meaningful relationships, yet the moment sin entered the world, these relationships took a turn for the worse. On the day Adam and Eve first disobeyed God, we find them arguing with one another and pointing fingers of blame at each other, all the while shifting uncomfortably beneath their fig-leaf underwear. One generation later, jealousy so poisoned the relationship between two of Adam and Eve's sons that one killed the other. Nothing has changed since the dawn of time. God made us to spend our lives interconnected with one another, yet we struggle just to get along. I don't know about you, but I find that relationships would be a breeze if it weren't for people. As Jerry Seinfeld once said, people are the worst.[9]

When God reconciled us to himself through his Son he also tore down the barriers that separate us from one another. Through the cross of Christ, God did away with everything that people cling to as excuses to hate. "In Christ's family there can be no division into Jew and non-Jew, slave and free, male and female. Among us you are all equal. That is, we are all in a common relationship with Jesus Christ," Paul wrote in Galatians 3:28. This isn't just some religious concept, but an expression of the lifestyle God makes possible among his children through his Spirit. The new life he gives us in Christ leads to new relationships between those of us who, on a natural level, may well have despised one another. As Paul also wrote, "Now we look inside, and what we see is that anyone united with the Messiah gets a fresh start, is created new. The old life is gone; a new life burgeons! Look at it! All this comes from the God who settled the relationship between us and him, and then called us to settle our relationships with each other" (2 Corinthians 5:17-18).

Far more than merely giving us the ability to connect by removing the walls that divided us, God made it essential that we do so by intertwining the life of each believer with the lives of every other. First Corinthians 12 compares this interrelationship to that of the various parts of the human body. According to the Bible, our lives are as connected and interdependent with those of other believers as our eyes are connected and interdependent with our stomachs. We can't declare our independence from other believers any more than an eye can wake up one day and decide it doesn't need anyone but itself, pluck itself out of the head, and go on its merry way. Every part of the body needs every other part to function at peak efficiency, even those parts we sometimes have to live without. My gallbladder decided to go on strike a few years ago. The rest of my body took a vote and decided it was time for Mr. Gallbladder to hit the road. I get along without it, although I feel the effects of its absence on a regular basis. I often think about my dearly departed gallbladder as I lay on the couch, holding my aching stomach, wishing my gallbladder was back inside happily doing what it was supposed to do.

MAKING THE CONNECTION   So what does this have to do with anything else in this book? Everything. The connections we form with other believers are the places where much of the process of owning your faith transpires. I know this may sound like a bit of a contradiction, since this entire book is built on the idea that your faith must be more than an extension of your pastor's or girlfriend's or parent's belief system. However, there is a huge difference between the interconnection God designed for his children, and the dependence on someone else as the source of your faith. In the latter, your mom or dad or pastor does all the heavy lifting of exploring the truths of the Bible and reconciling them with the world around them. Essentially, they believe for you. You're just along for the ride. That kind of faith won't last, because it isn't real faith at all. True believing demands making God and his eternal truths your own.

Yet God never meant for us to have to figure this out on our own. In many ways, Christianity is a communal faith. While we must make our own decision to follow Christ, the moment we do, we become part of a community and family that stretches back through time to the very first believers and across space to every other believer on every part of the globe. This means that we are not alone as we wrestle with the questions that push our faith to the edge. Those who came before us wrestled with many of these questions, and those who surround us are trying to make sense of the same issues. The process of making your faith your own involves listening to their voices and learning from their experiences.

All of this is a roundabout way of saying we need more than

a mind and a Bible as we make our way through the minefields that lie ahead of us. We need the wisdom of the entire Christian community. Talking to your peers about God is important, but it is also vital to step outside of your circle of friends. Listen to the voices of those who have traveled down this path longer than you have. Learn from the experiences of people like your pastor, your small group leaders, even your parents and grandparents.

Also listen to the wisdom contained in the rich library of learning handed down to you through two thousand years of believers struggling to cling to Christ in a fallen world. Reading the Bible is vital, but so is the reading of quality books. I don't know where I would be without C. S. Lewis, Charles Colson, or Francis Schaeffer. Their works have helped me gain a deeper understanding of God, while stretching my mind and forcing me to think through my faith in ways I would never have experienced on my own. Thomas à Kempis's book *The Imitation of Christ* has enriched my devotional life. Walter Kaiser and Gordon Fee opened up the Bible for me, while Max Lucado's *In the Grip of Grace* personalized the book of Romans and all Jesus did for me. Deitrich Bonhoeffer's *Life Together* transformed my understanding of Christian community, and Charles Swindoll's *Laugh Again* helped me regain the joy of following Christ. Yes, this is *my* faith. Yet my understanding of it is enriched by the rest of this community of believers.

The more I learn, the more I understand that the Christian faith does not begin anew with each generation. Instead, our understanding builds on those who came before us. That is why we must engage in a conversation with people and books that will push us to explore the nature of God. Did you get that? Engage in conversation. Don't just swallow whatever you hear without thinking. That will leave you more dazed and confused than you would be if you sat around watching SportsCenter all day. Instead, as you think through your faith, as you anchor it in the truth of the Bible and make it your own, allow the rest of Christ's body, your fellow believers, to help you on your journey.

LIFE TOGETHER You may have noticed that, except in passing, I haven't addressed all the moral decisions you will face on the typical college campus. I suppose I could, but in my mind I keep going back to a single command that I believe tells you all you need to know to make the right choices in any situation you might face. Deuteronomy 6:5 says, "Love GOD, your God, with your whole heart: love him with all that's in you, love him with all you've got!" When it comes to all the hard lifestyle decisions you will face, not only during college, but for the rest of your life, your choices ultimately come back to this: Whatever you do, it must express your love for God.

I know, I know. You want something a little more concrete. A student at a nearby college told me the other day, "Just once I wish someone would actually give me answers to these questions, rather than telling me how I can figure them out on my own." Fair enough. I can do that. I hereby give you the one concrete, set-in-stone rule that will deliver the right answer to every moral decision you will ever face: "Walk in the Spirit, and there is no way you will give in to the burning desires of your flesh" (Galatians 5:16, PAR). If you are a Christ follower, God's Spirit dwells inside of you. As you submit your will to his leadership, he will guide your path. This new life in Christ isn't about following rules, but about a love relationship with your Father in heaven. His Spirit brings this relationship down to a very personal level — one that changes the way you will live your day-to-day life.

As I write this in my backyard in Indiana, I can almost hear the howls of protest. How can I reduce all that can be said about the minefield of moral decisions you now face down to one simple sentence? The answer cannot be that easy. Yet the Bible says it is. Galatians 5:19-21 goes on to say:

> It is obvious what kind of life develops out of trying to get your own way all the time: repetitive, loveless, cheap sex; a stinking accumulation of mental and emotional garbage; frenzied and joyless grabs for happiness; trinket gods; magic-show religion; paranoid loneliness; cutthroat competition; all-consuming-yet-never-satisfied wants; a brutal temper; an impotence to love or be loved; divided homes and divided lives; small-minded and lopsided pursuits; the vicious habit of depersonalizing everyone into a rival; uncontrolled and uncontrollable addictions; ugly parodies of community. I could go on.

A long list of rules cannot keep these desires in check, nor can they stir up the kind of life that will please God. Only God's Spirit living inside of you can pull this off, which is exactly what he does. That is why I can so brazenly claim that all the answers you will ever need to the moral questions you face every day can be found in the act of walking in the Spirit of God. When you walk in him, you cannot possibly give in to the desires of your sinful nature.

All of this brings us back to the communal nature of the Christian faith. Christ's Spirit doesn't just dwell in you, but in every member of God's family. When we get together with other believers, the Lord himself is there in our midst (see Matthew 18:20). Therefore, the best and easiest way to walk in the Spirit is to stay close to others in whom the Holy Spirit dwells. This also means that the best way to make wise choices that will result in a lifestyle that pleases God and puts him on display in the most positive light, is to allow your life to stay interconnected with others who love God and want to serve him. As you make your way through the gauntlet of moral choices, you need friends who love the Lord and will care enough about you to notice if you start slipping away. Together, you are to encourage one another (see Hebrews 10:25), strengthen one another (see 1 Thessalonians 5:14), and serve one another (see Galatians 5:14). More than anything, you need someone who will love you enough to get in your face when you need it (see Galatians 2:11-14).

This is the obvious chapter, and the single most obvious expression of the Christian faith is to love other believers and to back up that love with action. Jesus himself said, "This is how everyone will recognize that you are my disciples—when they see the love you have for each other" (John 13:35). It wasn't good for Adam to be alone, and it isn't for you either. Christianity is a communal faith. Entrusting your life to Christ will unavoidably cause your life to become intertwined with others who have made the same commitment.

AN ARMY OF ONE DOESN'T WIN MANY WARS

CHAPTER 12

FROM THE TIME SHE was a little girl, Beth loved the theater. Pursuing it as a career was the only thing she could ever imagine doing. That's why she chose the university at which she applied and was accepted. They had one of the best musical theater departments in the Midwest, and the school was the perfect size for her. Attending a play during an on-campus visit late in her junior year of high school only solidified her decision. This was the school for her. It had everything she had ever wanted in a college.

Not long after she sent in her housing deposit, Beth started having second thoughts, not about the school, but about her choice of a major. During her next couple of campus visits, she met more theater majors, and she realized that her personality and perspectives didn't match theirs. Although she'd never been able to see herself doing anything else, she began to wonder if the theater was really for her. After much prayer and deliberation, she decided it wasn't.

After she changed her intended major, Beth thought about changing schools. Her university of choice may have had a strong theater program, but its English department—her new intended major—was both small and ordinary. Not only would a bigger school closer to her home offer a more heralded English department, it would also offer more choices if Beth decided to change majors again. On top of that, she had friends at the schools closer to home. At her school of choice, she would be alone in a different state, three and a half hours away from everything familiar.

In the end, she didn't change, because she was convinced God had led her to choose this university. By this point she wasn't sure why, but she was convinced that this college was God's will for her life. So, in the third week of August, her parents loaded her stuff in the back of their minivan and deposited her on a campus where she barely knew a soul. She'd met her roommate and a few other incoming freshmen at freshmen orientation in June, but that was about it. Once her parents and sisters climbed back into the van and headed toward home, Beth was alone in a strange place. Like the thousands of other students who go off to colleges far from home every year, Beth found herself in a position where she had to decide who she truly was. She had what she'd always considered to be a strong commitment to the Lord. Now she would find out how strong it really was.

Commitments are hard to keep when you are by yourself. That's why Beth breathed a sigh of relief when Jill, who lived in the dorm room across the hall from hers, walked over and introduced herself while Beth unpacked. Not only had both of them moved three and a half hours from home to a school where they didn't know anyone, but they also shared a mutual desire to walk with Christ. Solomon wrote in Ecclesiastes, "It's better to have a partner than go it alone. . . . With a friend you can face the worst" (4:9,12). Over the next few weeks, as Beth and Jill got to know one another, they discovered Solomon knew what he was talking about. The two of them encouraged each other and helped each other grow in their commitments to Jesus. To this day, neither one of them feels that their meeting was a coincidence. Instead, each sees the other as an answer to prayer.

SOMEONE TO LEAN ON   Talking about the communal elements of the Christian faith and the way God intertwines our lives together as believers comes down, on its most basic level, to two students in a dorm on a campus known for its parties, helping one another grow closer to God. This kind of relationship goes deeper than a usual friendship, because it is based on something greater than shared interests. It's not just hanging out with someone who lives next door who happens to like the Yankees or Julia Roberts movies. It's connecting with one who becomes like a brother or sister, because that's what he or she is. In his letter to the Galatians, Paul referred to the community of all the followers of Jesus as "Christ's family" (3:28). Not only do all believers share a relationship with the Father in heaven, we're all now connected as brothers and sisters. Like I've said about so many things before, this is more than religious talk. In Christ, our relationships with one another can grow deeper and hold stronger than even biological family relationships.

You need a friend like this to make it on your journey toward truly owning your faith. I know I did. Although I grew up in church and made a personal decision to follow Christ as a child, I never grew much beyond the basics. During my senior year of high school, I ran from God, but he reeled me back in. And he used one of my friends to do it. Like me, Steve had grown up in church and claimed to be a Christian. But neither of us lived it, and we did a lot of our "not living it" together. God intervened in both our lives, and the two of us turned back to him within a couple of weeks of one another. I can't really say how or why, since neither of us said anything about it then or since, but our relationship changed. We still water skied three or four times a week, but the conversations in the boat were different. You could say we held one another accountable, but that sounds much too formal. Looking back, I would say that we watched out for one another spiritually. I'd tried to clean up my act several times before, but this time was different. A large part of this difference came down to my friendship with Steve.

The friendships that God uses to help you take possession of your faith need two qualities in abundance: honesty and vulnerability. You need someone with whom you can completely be yourself. All of us have rough edges that don't become smooth all at once. Friends like this don't act shocked when your rough edges rub up against them. At the same time, they don't just stand by and pretend you're fine and nothing needs to change, when you both know it does. They're the kind of friends who will hold your hair while you're throwing up as a result of a bad decision, but who, the next day, don't hold back from telling you to get your act together. Solomon had this kind of friendship in mind when he wrote, "The heartfelt counsel of a friend is as sweet as perfume and incense" (Proverbs 27:9, NLT).

Vulnerability goes hand-in-hand with honesty. Within these friendships, you open up your true self, which is both necessary and frightening. It's also a reciprocal thing. Everyone would like to find someone who won't act shocked when they see us for who we truly are, but not many of us want to see beyond the veneer that others hide behind. But we must, for we don't just see what sits in front of us. According to Paul,

> Because of this decision we don't evaluate people by what they have or how they look. We looked at the Messiah

that way once and got it all wrong, as you know. We
certainly don't look at him that way anymore. Now we
look inside, and what we see is that anyone united with
the Messiah gets a fresh start, is created new. The old life
is gone; a new life burgeons! Look at it! (2 Corinthians
5:16-17)

The ability to see one another in light of our new lives in
Christ makes vulnerability possible. Friends who move you to
new levels of spiritual maturity are able to see the new creation
that God made of you when you surrendered your will to him.
More than that, they work to help you become who Christ
would have you be, rather than who you once were without him.
Obviously, relationships like this don't happen overnight, nor
can they be found with just anyone. They take time and trust.
Yet without them we are in danger of falling prey to the Elijah
syndrome.

NOT ALONE   Elijah was one of the greatest prophets who ever
lived. He stood up for the Lord during ancient Israel's darkest
days; he went against a corrupt king, a pagan queen, and a population that couldn't make up its mind about whether it would
serve the Lord or the pantheon of other gods at its disposal. But
standing alone eventually took its toll. Not long after a climactic
showdown with the prophets of the false god Baal, Elijah fled
for his life into the desert. Physically, emotionally, and spiritually exhausted, he sat down under a bush and prayed, "Enough of
this, GOD! Take my life—I'm ready to join my ancestors in the
grave!" (1 Kings 19:4). When God asked him to explain himself,
Elijah told him, "I've been working my heart out for the GOD-
of-the-Angel-Armies. . . . The people of Israel have abandoned

your covenant, destroyed the places of worship, and murdered your prophets. *I'm the only one left*, and now they're trying to kill me" (1 Kings 19:10, emphasis added).

Elijah wasn't just physically tired. He was tired of standing up alone. As far as he could see, no one else even cared about the Lord God. In the words of Romans 3:18, the people of Elijah's era never gave "God the time of day," even though they as a nation claimed to have a special relationship with him.

When party season breaks out on your college campus, you can feel a lot like Elijah. A recent ABC News report found that nearly half of all college students binge drink.[10] Again, I know alcohol was a problem on your high school campus. But in many colleges, the on-campus social life revolves around alcohol. If you aren't a partier, you don't fit in. When you live miles away from everything familiar, going against the tide accentuates the loneliness you can already feel.

When Elijah broke down, he told God that he couldn't keep on with his solo prophet gig. He needed a sign that someone, anyone, actually cared about doing the right thing for the right reason. God replied, "Meanwhile, I'm preserving for myself seven thousand souls: the knees that haven't bowed to the god Baal, the mouths that haven't kissed his image" (1 Kings 19:18). This was God's way of telling Elijah he wasn't alone. The Lord also directed Elijah to connect with a farmer named Elisha, who ultimately succeeded him as God's primary spokesman to Israel (see 19:15-17).

You may feel like the only genuine believer on your campus, but God has others who love him nearby. Since he is God, he is able to make your paths cross. Pray for it. Seek them out. Almost without exception, these others will also be students who are going through the same struggles you now face. The key is in knowing where to look. On-campus Christian ministries like The Navigators, InterVarsity Christian Fellowship, and Campus Crusade for Christ are good places to start. We will take a closer look at the impact these groups can have on your walk in the next chapter. Many denominations also have campus outreaches, such as the Southern Baptist Convention's Baptist Collegiate Ministries, and the Assemblies of God's Chi Alpha Campus Ministries. Most of these ministries have some sort of welcome activities planned at the beginning of every school year. You can also find a list of campus Christian ministries on your college's website or from your local church.

Beth got involved in an on-campus ministry at her college, which expanded her base of Christian friends at school. Yet the most important friendship she made during her first week of living on campus came seemingly quite by accident. Long before she ever arrived on campus, God knew the kind of friend she would need as she struggled to take possession of her faith. Philippians 4:19 promises, "You can be sure that God will take care of everything you need, his generosity exceeding even yours in the glory that pours from Jesus." Beth and Jill both found that God was faithful as he provided the friendship they needed when they needed it the most. He can and will do the same for you.

BIGGER THAN YOURSELF

CHAPTER 13

NOW I START TO sound like a parent. I saved it for the very end, but you knew it had to come out eventually. After all, I am a parent. My wife and I have three daughters who fit the profile of this book's target audience. So if what follows sounds like another parental lecture, I apologize ahead of time. It was inevitable.

Except, and this is what makes the tone of this chapter really bizarre, what follows is not a lecture I delivered to my daughters as they moved away to college. Quite the opposite. I wouldn't have approached this subject in this book, except that my girls told me it needed to be in here. They are the ones who, when I asked what factors made the biggest difference in taking ownership of their faith while at college, started talking about finding a church and getting involved in on-campus ministries. Go ahead and attach the polygraph wires if you like, but my story will not change. This chapter, in which I sound most like a parent, is in fact the shared advice delivered to me by two of my girls. They both said that one of the key factors in finalizing the process of making your faith your own is going beyond yourself and connecting with a group of other believers. And one way of doing this, of course, is by going to church.

MORE THAN RED BRICKS AND A STEEPLE In the interest of full disclosure, I need to tell you that my daughters grew up in church. My wife and I took each one of them for the first time when they were a couple of weeks old. From that moment forward, they attended on a regular basis. When you grow up in the home of a pastor, you can pretty much expect that. Even though I changed careers in 2002, we continued going to church together as a family. So you could say that my daughters went out and found a church after moving away to college because going to church is ingrained into their DNA. When you've done something every week for the first eighteen years of your life, you tend to keep on doing it.

Except we both know better. Attending church while growing up won't keep you coming back when you move away from home. A 2004 study released by the Higher Education Research Institute at UCLA found that, in 2000, 80 percent of college freshmen said they attended church frequently or occasionally in high school. Once they arrived on a college campus for their freshman year, the number dropped to 52 percent. By their junior year only 29 percent of students continued attending church frequently or occasionally.[11]

The statistics reflect the fact that attending church while in college takes a great deal of effort, not the least of which is letting the alarm clock win the battle on a day when your body screams to sleep in. On top of this, when you walk into a church as a single student, you suddenly find yourself in a completely different demographic from the one in which you grew up. The average church is geared toward families. You'll hear lots of sermons on how to be a better parent or how to be a better spouse, but you'll rarely hear one on how to deal with the pressures of living single. Then there's the sick feeling that washes over most of us at the thought of walking into a strange place where we don't know anyone. Eating out by yourself is no fun, but it can feel like a trip to Six Flags compared to sitting through a church service without having a soul speak to you. No wonder so many people find it easier to sleep in on Sunday mornings.

Faced with so many obstacles, why should you pass on that extra can of Red Bull at midnight on Saturday, drag yourself out of bed on Sunday morning, and go find a church to call your own? To understand the answer, you need to look beyond the building and the sermons and the programs and see the church the way God sees it. The New Testament places the church at the center of God's activity on earth today. In God's eyes, his church is the "pillar and support of the truth" (1 Timothy 3:15, NLT). In Ephesians Paul says Christ loved the church so much that he gave his life for it (see 5:25, NLT). Jesus said that he would establish his church and make it "so expansive with energy that not even the gates of hell will be able to keep it out" (Matthew 16:18). This church is Christ's body (see Colossians 1:24, NLT), and he is its head. Each local congregation is an extension of his body. In a very real sense, every local church is the arms and legs of Jesus, completing the work he started while he was on the earth (see 1 Corinthians 12; Acts 1:1).

Woody Allen once said that 80 percent of success is just showing up, but you need to do more than just show up at church to experience all that God wants to accomplish through the role of the church in your life. I know, I know, I'm starting to sound like a parent again. Next thing you know, I'll be telling you to eat more green vegetables and go to bed at a decent hour. What's next, a lecture on how you should find a church where you can volunteer to help in the Wednesday night children's program or to deliver meals to senior adults on Saturday afternoons? Why don't I go all the way and tell you that church is not about what you get out of it, but what you put into it?

Wow. Rereading that last sentence made me think my mother hacked into my computer and started writing this book for me.

But my mother didn't tell me this, my daughters did. They learned on their own what I, too, had to figure out for myself a couple of hundred years ago when I was in college. They told me they didn't want to find some place where they could kill an hour singing songs and listening to a sermon. If that's all church involved, they figured they would just as soon not bother. I doubt if they realized it, but their decision to look for more was a major decision in making their faith their own. It may not seem like a big deal, but it is.

When you were a kid, decisions like which church to attend were made for you. Even if you picked a different church from your parents, or went without them, you probably chose a church based on where your friends went or on which church had a happening youth ministry. However, as you take ownership of your faith, you now have to ask yourself not only which church will you attend, but why you want to go at all. If you simply look for the one that offers the best entertainment value—that is, the one that has the best band, the biggest and best collegiate ministry, or the most entertaining preacher—you're still missing the point of what this faith is all about. Taking ownership of your faith means taking a close look at what the church teaches and how that compares to the Bible. You also need to explore opportunities for hands-on ministries. And since this entire section of the book is on connecting with others, you need to look for a place that offers the kind of diversity you cannot find in the bubble that is most college campuses. As you make the decision to allow your life to become intertwined with the lives of others through a church, you set the stage for your life after college. This won't be the last time you have to decide whether or not you will be a part of Christ's body here on earth.

WHAT TO LOOK FOR   I guess since I'm already being so parental in this chapter, I should give you some practical, parental advice on what to look for in a church. Looking for a church isn't like shopping for a used car. The key issue is not what a church has to offer you, although many people approach finding a church in this way. In fact, when it comes to finding the right place to connect spiritually, *you* aren't even the key part of the equation. The question isn't which church is right for you, but where does God want to use your unique blend of gifts, talents, and perspectives. Paul said that "God has carefully placed each part of the body right where he wanted it" (1 Corinthians 12:18). Therefore, as you look for a church, you need to ask him where he wants to place you.

As you begin your search for God's answers, there are some essentials you should watch for. First and foremost, find a church that bases its teachings and practices on the Bible. To be fair, I've yet to see a church that advertised itself as unbiblical in its teachings and practices. Even Jehovah's Witnesses claim to teach and practice the Bible, even though they deny the key elements of Christianity, such as Jesus' deity, salvation by grace alone, and the triune nature of God. The only way you can know if a church is truly aligned with the Bible is to read it for yourself, which of course, you're already doing, since you've read section two of this book.

Second, look for a church that balances the different purposes of the church. My first staff position was at a church that excelled in evangelism. Every day the pastor came up with new and inventive ways to reach out to people who couldn't care less about God. His ideas usually worked. Each week more and more people made first-time commitments to follow Christ. However, the church didn't do a very good job of equipping these new believers for a lifetime of walking with Christ. I once had a man complain, "This is a great place for baby Christians, but after you've been at it for a couple of years, you probably need to go somewhere else to keep growing." Look for a church that balances reaching people with teaching them how to grow in Christ, as well as with God's other purposes for his church, such as worship, ministry, and missions.

Third, and like any good parent I am now about to repeat something I've already said (but aren't all parental lectures reruns?), look for a place that will give you opportunities to do hands-on ministry. Volunteer to help in the nursery or to work with kids in Awana or some other children's ministry. If kids aren't your forte, find something that is. Every church has needs you can fill. Look for one that gives you the opportunity to dive in and get your hands dirty.

Finally, as you search for just the right place, guard yourself against the Dorothy syndrome, so named for Dorothy Gale of *The Wizard of Oz* fame. Dorothy spent so much time clicking her heels, chanting that there was no place like home, that she never learned to appreciate the sheer Oziness of Oz. I've been to Kansas. Oz looks way cooler than a bunch of flat land covered with wheat and sunflowers. There may be no place like your home church, either, but don't let that keep you from investing your life in someplace new. I've always looked at finding a church as a little like eating Aunt Bea's pickles (with apologies to those of you who aren't fans of *The Andy Griffith Show* and therefore won't understand the analogy). If you look hard enough you can find something not to like about any place. Ultimately, you just have to choose one and learn to love it. That doesn't mean the first place you visit will be the church you need to learn to love, nor does this mean that you must visit a half dozen or more before making up your mind. To be honest, there's nothing I dislike more than trying to find a new church home. However, like every other part of this journey of faith, through much prayer and surrender to the will of God, you will find that the Holy Spirit will guide you as you search for the place he has in store for you.

CONNECTING ON CAMPUS   If the guys who ran the on-campus ministries at the University of Tulsa during my freshman year happen to pick up this book, they will likely find what follows to be inconceivable (or maybe it would explain a few things they've always wondered about). I would send them a copy just for their reading pleasure, but I don't know who they are. My roommate and I were always too busy hiding from them to ever ask their names or recognize their faces. They would venture into John Mabee Hall every month or so to talk to pagans like me about the Lord. Before they could make it to the second floor, though, one of our fellow pagans would run down the halls screaming, "The Jesus guys are coming!" Every door on the floor would then slam shut and all the lights went out. Hiding silently in the dark, we would wait as the Jesus guys knocked on one door after another. Finally, an all clear signal would sound and we would all venture back out, like Helen Hunt and Bill Paxton climbing out from under a bridge in *Twister*. That was my experience with on-campus ministries while I lived in a dorm.

Now that I'm a parent, I don't want my children to hide from the Jesus people on campus. Far from it. When my oldest daughter called to say she'd become involved with the InterVarsity Christian Fellowship (IV) chapter on her campus, I was thrilled. More than thrilled. I thought this would be a good place for her to connect with other believers on campus, as well as give her a life outside of her dorm room. It took me a couple of years of observation to realize I'd made the mistake of looking at IV, Campus Crusade, The Navigators, and all the other on-campus ministries through the eyes of a consumer.

On-campus ministries shouldn't be approached with a what's-in-it-for-me attitude. They do offer a place to connect with other believers on campus. And most have weekly worship services and Bible studies and other activities geared toward helping you mature spiritually. However, the greatest value that I've observed goes to the core of what this book is all about. Over her four years in college, I watched as my oldest daughter not only attended IV, she also became involved in its leadership. She became a small group leader, joined the leadership team that planned the weekly large group meetings and occasional campus outreach events, and dove in wherever needed. She wasn't alone. Most on-campus ministries are designed to provide these kinds of opportunities to you. Not only do they help you take ownership of your faith, they give you an outlet to put your faith into action.

~

This brings us full circle. Owning your faith means developing an intimate relationship with Christ and expanding your understanding of his eternal truth. It moves you to serve and to connect with others. Ultimately, taking ownership means growing to a point where you can help others take ownership of their faith as well. I guess I could make one more overtly parental statement about how you are the future of Christianity. I will refrain. I've talked like a parent long enough for one chapter.

GOING DEEPER   To dive deeper, consider reading the following:

- Dietrich Bonhoeffer, *Life Together*
- Charles Colson, *Being the Body*
- Francis Schaeffer, *The Mark of the Christian* and *The Great Evangelical Disaster*

BE WHO YOU ARE

SOME FRIENDS ARE COMING over for dinner tomorrow night, but I'm not sure what to cook. Our friends are vegetarians. Well, sometimes. Sometimes they are vegans. They've also been known to go crazy on bacon. When the mood strikes, they can polish off a pound in one sitting. A couple of weeks ago my youngest daughter ran into our friends at Cracker Barrel. They were having fried chicken. Needless to say, planning the menu for tomorrow night is a little tricky. My wife planned on serving enchiladas, but we're not sure what kind to make. We're vacillating between chicken and cheese, neither of which will work if this is a vegan week. Do vegans eat enchiladas? I almost hate to ask.

I hesitate to call my friends bad vegetarians. They are, after all, my friends. Who am I, the committed carnivore, to condemn them? Since they sometimes eat meat, I'm not sure if they are still, technically, vegetarians at all. A more committed herbivore might get in their face and tell them to get with the vegetarian program. They would say that my friends' periodic wanderings toward the meat section of the Cracker Barrel menu give vegetarians everywhere a bad name. Me, I would say they live a vegetarianesque lifestyle — if vegetarianesque were a word, and my spell check tells me it's not. I'm hoping they're off the wagon this week. I prefer chicken enchiladas to cheese, and I prefer both to a tortilla wrapped around tofu covered with tofu sour cream.

My friends probably didn't abandon their vegetarian ways overnight. The process came about slowly over time. I would imagine that little things like the smell of bacon drifting through the local diner and the sizzle of steak on the grill during a family reunion whittled away at their resolve. I don't know what the statistics are for vegetarians falling off the wagon, but whatever they are, my friends are now part of them. The only way for them to escape that particular statistic trap is to decide who and what they really are. Vegetarian, vegan, or full-blown carnivore, they simply need to be who they are.

And so do you.

The worst fate that can befall you as a confessed Christ follower is not for you to fall away from God completely. In the eyes of God, a far more dangerous and seductive avenue lies before you, the path of a Christianesque lifestyle. Jesus complained of the church in Laodicea, "You're not cold, you're not hot — far better to be either cold or hot! You're stale. You're stagnant. You make me want to vomit" (Revelation 3:15-16). The problem was that the people of Laodicea had no idea their lives were so off target. They thought everything was great between them and God, never realizing that they'd lost their passion for him. Instead they'd settled into safe, Christianesque lives that made God sick.

The Christianesque lifestyle goes to two extremes, and in both you can feel like you have it all together spiritually. The first emphasizes keeping rules for God, also known as legalism. In this extreme, you show your devotion to Christ by the clothes you wear and how short you cut your hair, or, if you are a female, by not cutting it at all. If you are really serious, you won't watch television or go to movies or listen to any music wilder than Bill and Gloria Gaither. This approach appears to be commendable, yet when compared to the lifestyle the New Testament demands, it falls well short. Keeping rules is simple compared to the weightier issues of dying to oneself and following Christ.

The other Christianesque extreme leans heavily upon God's grace with the idea that, since God is in the forgiving business, it's best to throw a little business his way from time to time. With this approach, you feel like you have a special understanding with God. He knows you have needs and urges. After all, he made you that way. Giving in can't be that big of a deal. Other questions, like the words you use and your favorite recreational activities, fall under the umbrella of the freedom believers enjoy in Christ. When pressed, adherents of this approach acknowledge being Christians. Unfortunately, the silent testimonies of their lives leave much to be desired.

The solution isn't more rules. Or fewer rules. Or any rules at all. The real answer is to simply be who you are, or rather, to grow into the person God designed you to be by knowing, thinking, serving, and connecting. As you take ownership of your faith, let your faith take ownership of you. Paul put it this way, "I have been crucified with Christ: and I myself no longer live, but Christ lives in me. And the real life I now have within this body is a result of my trusting in the Son of God, who loved me and gave himself for me" (Galatians 2:20, TLB). This is the result of truly taking ownership of your faith.

And that is my final challenge to you. Be who you are. Let the Son of God, whose Spirit dwells within you, spill over into every aspect of your life. Grow in him as you let him grow in you. When all is said and done, this is the ultimate proof of whether or not you truly own your faith.

INTRODUCTION TO THE OWN YOUR FAITH DISCUSSION GUIDE

IT'S ONE THING TO read a book about owning your faith, but quite another really to own it. Use this discussion guide to help you think through the challenges in the book. You may find it helpful to use the guide with a group of people who, like you, are struggling to understand how to own their faith.

The guide is divided into four sections that correspond to the four sections of the book. Pause after you read each section and talk through the questions, or work through them yourself. Pray about them. Stick with them until you feel comfortable with the answers.

Don't be afraid to question everything—God is bigger than your biggest question!

OWN YOUR FAITH DISCUSSION GUIDE

GREG LIPPS

SECTION ONE: KNOW
Chapter 2: The Shortest Distance

FROM THE TEXT

In the midst of all our activity for God, our connection to him can be lost. Instead of approaching him directly, we try to perform for him, as if he will let us be close to him only if we prove ourselves worthy. This path won't take us any closer to God. Instead, it leads only to frustration.

THINK ABOUT IT

1. Do you ever find yourself so wrapped up in acting for God that you actually forget about God? What kind of an impact does that have on your spiritual walk?
2. God can be so intangible sometimes that we tend toward performing as a way to live out our relationship with him. How do we love something that we cannot see?

3. Does God expect us to feel love for him or just to act on the love we say we have?

Chapter 3: And on Thursday Night Everyone Got Saved (Again)

FROM THE TEXT

Making your faith your own doesn't just mean figuring out what you believe and why you believe it. Nor is it simply taking a stand for Christ when everyone else goes another direction. Your faith becomes your own when, in the silence, you can say with Peter, "Master, to whom would we go? You have the words of real life, eternal life" (John 6:68).

THINK ABOUT IT

1. How do we begin praying or even maintain a fruitful prayer life when we don't have the feel-good emotion we typically associate with our faith? (For help, read James 5:13-18.)
2. Do you think having a spiritual buzz equals salvation? Are those emotional highs important to our growth or are they just meaningless experiences?
3. If faith is not about emotions, then is it all an intellectual decision? What do you think is the balance in faith between emotion and intellect?

Chapter 4: Meet with Me

FROM THE TEXT

Most of our lives are filled with noise. From the music blaring from speakers or coming through our earbuds, to the television, to the constant flow of communication through phone calls, text messages, instant messages, and e-mails, an incessant stream of noise runs through our souls. Psalm 46:10 tells us to unplug, to silence ourselves and the noise around us, to step out of the traffic so we might know that God is God.

THINK ABOUT IT

1. What is your experience with being still before the Lord?
2. Have you ever seen God show up, either in a tangible or intangible way?
3. How do we fear God and love him at the same time? Practically, what does that look like?
4. What kind of changes should take place in your life when God shows up? What about in the body of Christ? What kind of changes should happen there?

SECTION TWO: THINK
Chapter 5: Question Everything

FROM THE TEXT

And everything means everything: Every idea you believe is true and every one you're sure is false—question them all. Pull out your beliefs about God, Jesus, the Bible, your ideas about the meaning of life, and even your beliefs about the way people showed up on this planet. Pull them all out of the recesses of your mind and ask, "Am I sure about this one?"

THINK ABOUT IT

1. What are some of your most deeply rooted convictions?
2. Are they the same as or different from your parents'?

3. Is there someone close to you who has been influential in forming them? If so, what role has that person's influence played?
4. Why do you stand by those convictions?

A BRIEF EXERCISE

Sigmund Freud, who was decidedly NOT a Christ follower, believed that "there are no sources of knowledge in the universe other than carefully scrutinized observations."[12] Compare that to C. S. Lewis, a theologian who believed that "if there was a controlling power outside the universe, . . . the only way in which we could expect it to show itself would be inside ourselves as an influence or command trying to get us to behave in a certain way. And that is just what we do find inside ourselves."[13]

Freud believed that we make up our moral code just as we make up our traffic laws. According to his view, our moral code persists only because it is intentionally and actively passed from parent to child, from one generation to the next. Lewis, on the other hand, says that God places this code in us to discover, as we discover the laws of mathematics, and that this universal moral law transcends time and culture. Read Romans 2:14-15 for a biblical viewpoint.

THINK ABOUT IT

1. Which viewpoint do you think is true?
2. If it is true, what are the logical implications?
3. If it is true, how must your life change to live it out?

Chapter 6: Immersed in Truth

FROM THE TEXT

Not only will reading be a vital part of the journey to make your faith your own, it also prepares you for the struggle of reconciling God's eternal truth with the ideas thrown your way every day in the classroom. With the Bible as your baseline of understanding, you are ready to think.

THINK ABOUT IT

1. Do you experience God when you read the Bible?
2. In what other settings do you encounter God's presence?
3. Do you believe the story of God found in the Bible to be the only foundation on which to build your understanding of creation? Are other stories useful in your quest to gain understanding of life?
4. Would you describe the Bible as a book of information or as a book about human formation? Why?

Chapter 7: I Had to Read a Book by Stephen Hawking for a
        Physics Class

FROM THE TEXT

Proper preparation is the key to surviving the inevitable storms that will confront your faith. . . . The difference between being told what to think and learning how to think is the difference between a faith that is your own and one that is nothing more than an extension of those who programmed your mind.

THINK ABOUT IT

1. Do you believe in the authority of Jesus?
2. Do you need anything more on which to base your decisions? If so, what?
3. Is the authority of the Bible sufficient for you when dealing with ambiguous issues? For example, would you work on a Sunday if your boss required it? Why or why not?
4. Brooke Foss Westcott (1825-1901) wrote, "Truth seen as truth carries with it condemnation to all who refuse to welcome it."[14] What does that mean to you?

A BRIEF EXERCISE

Modern society presents many challenges to your faith. Among these is the issue of the sanctity of life. One well-known case garnered national attention when the husband of Terri Schiavo disagreed with her parents about ending life support for the severely brain-damaged woman. The courts eventually sided with the husband and refused to order a feeding tube to be reinserted, thereby setting in motion the events that eventually ended her life.[15]

Mark says that when we are approached with a challenge to our faith we should build on the baseline, keep an open mind, know our limitations, and search for truth. With that in mind, how would you approach the Terri Schiavo dilemma?

SECTION THREE: **SERVE**
Chapter 8: The Fine Print

FROM THE TEXT

I've also learned that the grand adventure days are, in truth-in-advertising terms, not typical of the day-to-day business of ministry. If they were, sticking with the work of being a servant for Christ would be easy. It isn't. Becoming a servant will provide a constant source of testing for your faith.

A BRIEF EXERCISE

Take a look at 2 Corinthians 5:14-15 for more insight into a life of service for Christ. Then consider the words William Barclay wrote:

> Work well done rises like a hymn of praise to God. This means that the doctor on his rounds, the scientist in his laboratory, the teacher in his classroom, the musician at his music, the artist at his canvas, the shop assistant at his counter, the typist at her typewriter, the housewife in her kitchen—all who are doing the work of the world as it should be done are joining in a great act of worship.[16]

THINK ABOUT IT

1. Is it enough to do our daily assigned tasks, "as to the Lord"? (Ephesians 6:7, KJV). Will God really send us out like the goats in Matthew 25:32-46 if we do not step out and do more?
2. An old maxim says that charity begins at home. So, is it acceptable that we use our limited time to take care

of our families? Isn't that enough? Do we really need to seek out other opportunities to serve?

Chapter 9: Muddy Hands

FROM THE TEXT

The Son of God, the One who spoke the galaxies into existence, stands in front of me with dirty hands. . . . Taking hold of Jesus' muddy hand and joining him in serving others is the third step in making your faith your own. In fact, it ultimately is the test of whether or not your faith is real at all. . . . When we truly understand what Jesus is all about, when his love for us takes hold of our hearts and this faith becomes who we are, we will become a servant whether we receive any tangible benefits or not. . . . Dirty-hands ministry is the natural result of living a life that has ceased to be about you.

THINK ABOUT IT

1. What are some tangible, realistic ways we can serve others?
2. Can we ever serve enough? Can we ever serve too much?
3. How would your life change if, in every decision you made, you put the Kingdom of God first?

    - What would you eat?
    - What would you wear?
    - Where would you live?
    - What kind of car would you drive?
    - What school would you attend?
    - What career would you pursue?

Chapter 10: From the Core

FROM THE TEXT

Everyone who receives new life in Christ can no longer live a self-serving, self-indulgent lifestyle. That doesn't mean we are incapable of self-absorption or that putting others before ourselves comes naturally. However, when the Holy Spirit takes up residence inside of us, he reshapes our desires. When we understand both mentally and experientially that Jesus loves us more than our minds can ever comprehend, we will want to love him back by loving those who bear his image.

THINK ABOUT IT

1. Mark described his friend Greg, who works tirelessly for the Lord. But isn't he really an exception? Is everyone called to do things the way Greg did them?
2. Is it possible to be enthusiastic for the Lord and still be considered cool?
3. The world can sometimes be a dark and scary place. What are some ways you can hold onto hope while acknowledging the way things really are?

SECTION FOUR: CONNECT

Chapter 11: The Obvious Chapter

FROM THE TEXT

We can't declare our independence from other believers any more than an eye can wake up one day and decide it doesn't need anyone but itself, pluck itself out of the head, and go on its merry way. . . . It wasn't good for Adam to be alone, and it isn't for you either. Christianity is a communal faith. Entrusting your life to Christ will unavoidably cause your life to become intertwined with others who have made the same commitment. Look at the way Paul emphasizes this point in Philippians 2:1–11.

THINK ABOUT IT

1. How does God make it possible for us to get along in community?
2. Have you experienced a genuine Christian community? If so, what does it mean to you? If not, what have you been missing out on?
3. Albert Einstein said, "Two things are infinite: the universe and human stupidity; and I'm not sure about the universe." When you encounter people who are hard to deal with, what are some ways you can maintain healthy relationships?

Chapter 12: An Army of One Doesn't Win Many Wars

FROM THE TEXT

The friendships that God uses to help you take possession of your faith need two qualities in abundance: honesty and vulnerability. You need someone with whom you can completely be yourself.

THINK ABOUT IT

1. What do you do when you are lonely?
2. When was the last time you had an honest, heart-to-heart discussion with someone? Describe what that was like and if it had any effect on you.

3. Do you have a friend with whom you can be vulnerable? If not, in what ways would your life have to change if you had one?

4. Rate the following statements from one to three, with one being you often feel that way and three being you never feel that way:

- People won't love me if they know what I'm really like.
- People will think I'm not a "good Christian" if they know the real me.
- People don't really care about me.
- I'm afraid people will talk about me behind my back.

What drives you to feel the way you do?

5. What are some ways you can begin to develop more positive friendships in your life? Where can you go to find those people?

Chapter 13: Bigger Than Yourself

FROM THE TEXT

One of the key factors in finalizing the process of making your faith your own is going beyond yourself and connecting with a group of other believers.

THINK ABOUT IT

1. Do you think it is important to your spiritual growth to attend a traditional church, or is it okay to simply be in a community of believers? Do you attend a church?

Why or why not?

2. What are the things that make a church "good"?

3. What are some things you would definitely not want to see in church?

4. In what kinds of ministries do you think you would be most effective?

5. Rob Bell, pastor of Mars Hill church and author of *Velvet Elvis: Repainting the Christian Faith* wrote,

> Remember what Jesus always wanted to know? He asked, "What's the fruit we're producing? Is justice being done? Are people sharing their possessions? Are the oppressed being set free? Are relationships being healed?" To me, that's the point. Everything else is just chatter.

Do you agree or disagree? And if you agree, what does that truth mean for the way you live your life from here on?

~

GOING DEEPER

If you and your group are looking for more ways to own your faith, consider choosing one of the books mentioned earlier and reading through it together. When you're done, make up and talk about discussion questions that fit your lives. Remember, you're never done growing!

A SCHEDULE TO READ THROUGH THE BIBLE IN ONE YEAR

APPENDIX A

1.	Genesis 1–2	Matthew 1
2.	Genesis 3–5	Matthew 2
3.	Genesis 6–8	Matthew 3
4.	Genesis 9–11	Matthew 4
5.	Genesis 12–14	Matthew 5:1-20
6.	Genesis 15–17	Matthew 5:21-48

7.	**Reflect**

8.	Genesis 18–20	Matthew 6:1-18
9.	Genesis 21–23	Matthew 6:19-34
10.	Genesis 24–26	Matthew 7:1-14
11.	Genesis 27–29	Matthew 7:15-29
12.	Genesis 30–32	Matthew 8:1-17
13.	Genesis 33–35	Matthew 8:18-34

14.	**Reflect**

15.	Genesis 36–38	Matthew 9:1-17
16.	Genesis 39–41	Matthew 9:18-38
17.	Genesis 42–44	Matthew 10
18.	Genesis 45–47	Matthew 11
19.	Genesis 48–50	Matthew 12:1-21
20.	Exodus 1–2	Matthew 12:22-50

21.	**Reflect**

22.	Exodus 3–5	Matthew 13:1-35
23.	Exodus 6–8	Matthew 13:36-58
24.	Exodus 9–11	Matthew 14
25.	Exodus 12–14	Matthew 15:1-20
26.	Exodus 15–17	Matthew 15:21-39
27.	Exodus 18–20	Matthew 16

28. Reflect

29.	Exodus 21–23	Matthew 17
30.	Exodus 24–27	Matthew 18:1-20
31.	Exodus 28–31	Matthew 18:21-35
32.	Exodus 32–34	Matthew 19
33.	Exodus 35–37	Matthew 20
34.	Exodus 38–40	Matthew 21:1-22

35. Reflect

36.	Leviticus 1–3	Matthew 21:23-46
37.	Leviticus 4–7	Matthew 22:1-22
38.	Leviticus 8–10	Matthew 22:23-46
39.	Leviticus 11–12	Matthew 23
40.	Leviticus 13–15	Matthew 24:1-22
41.	Leviticus 16–17	Matthew 24:23-51

42. Reflect

43.	Leviticus 18–20	Matthew 25:1-30
44.	Leviticus 21–23	Matthew 25:31-46
45.	Leviticus 24–25	Matthew 26:1-30
46.	Leviticus 26–27	Matthew 26:31-75
47.	Numbers 1–2	Matthew 27
48.	Numbers 3–5	Matthew 28

49. Reflect

50.	Numbers 6–8	Mark 1:1-28
51.	Numbers 9–12	Mark 1:29-45
52.	Numbers 13–14	Mark 2
53.	Numbers 15–17	Mark 3
54.	Numbers 18–20	Mark 4
55.	Numbers 21–24	Mark 5

56.	**Reflect**	
57.	Numbers 25–26	Mark 6:1-29
58.	Numbers 27–29	Mark 6:30-56
59.	Numbers 30–31	Mark 7
60.	Numbers 32–34	Mark 8:1–9:1
61.	Numbers 35–36	Mark 9:2-50
62.	Deuteronomy 1–2	Mark 10:1-34
63.	**Reflect**	
64.	Deuteronomy 3–4	Mark 10:35-52
65.	Deuteronomy 5–7	Mark 11
66.	Deuteronomy 8–10	Mark 12
67.	Deuteronomy 11–13	Mark 13
68.	Deuteronomy 14–16	Mark 14:1-42
69.	Deuteronomy 17–19	Mark 14:43-72
70.	**Reflect**	
71.	Deuteronomy 20–22	Mark 15
72.	Deuteronomy 23–25	Mark 16
73.	Deuteronomy 26–28	Luke 1:1-25
74.	Deuteronomy 29–31	Luke 1:26-80
75.	Deuteronomy 32–34	Luke 2
76.	Joshua 1–2	Luke 3
77.	**Reflect**	
78.	Joshua 3–5	Luke 4
79.	Joshua 6–8	Luke 5
80.	Joshua 9–12	Luke 6:1-26
81.	Joshua 13–15	Luke 6:27-49
82.	Joshua 16–18	Luke 7:1-35
83.	Joshua 19–21	Luke 7:36-50
84.	**Reflect**	
85.	Joshua 22–24	Luke 8:1-25
86.	Judges 1–3	Luke 8:26-56
87.	Judges 4–6	Luke 9:1-36
88.	Judges 7–9	Luke 9:37-62

89.	Judges 10–12	Luke 10
90.	Judges 13–14	Luke 11:1-28

91.	**Reflect**

92.	Judges 15–16	Luke 11:29-54
93.	Judges 17–18	Luke 12:1-34
94.	Judges 19–21	Luke 12:35-59
95.	1 Samuel 1–2	Luke 13
96.	1 Samuel 3–6:18	Luke 14
97.	1 Samuel 6:19–9	Luke 15

98.	**Reflect**

99.	1 Samuel 10–12	Luke 16
100.	1 Samuel 13–15	Luke 17
101.	1 Samuel 16–18	Luke 18
102.	1 Samuel 19–21	Luke 19
103.	1 Samuel 22–24	Luke 20:1-19
104.	1 Samuel 25–27	Luke 20:20-47

105.	**Reflect**

106.	1 Samuel 28–31	Luke 21
107.	2 Samuel 1–2	Luke 22:1-38
108.	2 Samuel 3–5	Luke 22:39-71
109.	2 Samuel 6–8	Luke 23
110.	2 Samuel 9–10	Luke 24
111.	2 Samuel 11–13	John 1:1-18

112.	**Reflect**

113.	2 Samuel 14–16	John 1:19-51
114.	2 Samuel 17–19	John 2
115.	2 Samuel 20–22	John 3
116.	2 Samuel 23–24	John 4
117.	1 Kings 1–2	John 5
118.	1 Kings 3–5	John 6:1-59

119.	**Reflect**

120.	1 Kings 6–7	John 6:60-71
121.	1 Kings 8	John 7:1-24

122.	1 Kings 9–11	John 7:25-53
123.	1 Kings 12–14	John 8:1-30
124.	1 Kings 15–17	John 8:31-58
125.	1 Kings 18–19	John 9

| **126.** | **Reflect** | |

127.	1 Kings 20–22	John 10
128.	2 Kings 1–2	John 11:1-37
129.	2 Kings 3–5	John 11:38-57
130.	2 Kings 6–7	John 12:1-36
131.	2 Kings 8–9	John 12:37-50
132.	2 Kings 10–11	John 13:1-17

| **133.** | **Reflect** | |

134.	2 Kings 12–14	John 13:18-38
135.	2 Kings 15–17	John 14
136.	2 Kings 18–19	John 15
137.	2 Kings 20–21	John 16
138.	2 Kings 22–23	John 17
139.	2 Kings 24–25	John 18:1-27

| **140.** | **Reflect** | |

141.	Isaiah 1–3	John 18:28-40
142.	Isaiah 4–6	John 19
143.	Isaiah 7–9	John 20:1-18
144.	Isaiah 10–12	John 20:19-31
145.	Isaiah 13–15	John 21
146.	Isaiah 16–18	Acts 1:1-11

| **147.** | **Reflect** | |

148.	Isaiah 19–21	Acts 1:12-26
149.	Isaiah 22–24	Acts 2
150.	Isaiah 25–27	Acts 3
151.	Isaiah 28–30	Acts 4
152.	Isaiah 31–33	Acts 5:1-11
153.	Isaiah 34–35	Acts 5:12-42

| **154.** | **Reflect** | |

155.	Isaiah 36–37	Acts 6
156.	Isaiah 38–39	Acts 7
157.	Isaiah 40–41	Acts 8:1-25
158.	Isaiah 42–43	Acts 8:26-40
159.	Isaiah 44–45	Acts 9:1-19
160.	Isaiah 46–48	Acts 9:20-43

161. Reflect

162.	Isaiah 49–51	Acts 10:1-23
163.	Isaiah 52–54	Acts 10:24-48
164.	Isaiah 55–57	Acts 11
165.	Isaiah 58–60	Acts 12
166.	Isaiah 61–63	Acts 13:1-13
167.	Isaiah 64–66	Acts 13:14-52

168. Reflect

169.	Jeremiah 1–2	Acts 14
170.	Jeremiah 3–5	Acts 15:1-21
171.	Jeremiah 6–8	Acts 15:22-41
172.	Jeremiah 9–11	Acts 16:1-15
173.	Jeremiah 12–14	Acts 16:16-40
174.	Jeremiah 15–17	Acts 17:1-15

175. Reflect

176.	Jeremiah 18–20	Acts 17:16-34
177.	Jeremiah 21–23	Acts 18
178.	Jeremiah 24–26	Acts 19:1-20
179.	Jeremiah 27–28	Acts 19:21-41
180.	Jeremiah 29–30	Acts 20:1-16
181.	Jeremiah 31–32	Acts 20:17-38

182. Reflect

183.	Jeremiah 33–35	Acts 21:1-25
184.	Jeremiah 36–38	Acts 21:26-40
185.	Jeremiah 39–41	Acts 22:1-29
186.	Jeremiah 42–44	Acts 22:30–23:11
187.	Jeremiah 45–47	Acts 23:12-35
188.	Jeremiah 48–49	Acts 24

189.	**Reflect**	
190.	Jeremiah 50–51	Acts 25
191.	Jeremiah 52	Acts 26
192.	Ezekiel 1–3	Acts 27:1-26
193.	Ezekiel 4–6	Acts 27:27-44
194.	Ezekiel 7–8	Acts 28
195.	Ezekiel 9–11	Romans 1:1-17

196.	**Reflect**	
197.	Ezekiel 12–14	Romans 1:18-32
198.	Ezekiel 15–17	Romans 2
199.	Ezekiel 18–20	Romans 3
200.	Ezekiel 21–22	Romans 4
201.	Ezekiel 23–24	Romans 5:1-11
202.	Ezekiel 25–27	Romans 5:12-21

203.	**Reflect**	
204.	Ezekiel 28–31	Romans 6
205.	Ezekiel 32–34	Romans 7
206.	Ezekiel 35–37	Romans 8:1-17
207.	Ezekiel 38–39	Romans 8:18-39
208.	Ezekiel 40–44	Romans 9
209.	Ezekiel 45–48	Romans 10

210.	**Reflect**	
211.	Hosea 1–4	Romans 11
212.	Hosea 5–9	Romans 12
213.	Hosea 10–14	Romans 13
214.	Joel	Romans 14
215.	Amos 1–3	Romans 15
216.	Amos 4–6	Romans 16

217.	**Reflect**	
218.	Amos 7–9	1 Corinthians 1
219.	Obadiah	1 Corinthians 2
220.	Jonah	1 Corinthians 3
221.	Micah 1–3	1 Corinthians 4

222.	Micah 4–7	1 Corinthians 5
223.	Nahum	1 Corinthians 6

224.	**Reflect**

225.	Habakkuk	1 Corinthians 7
226.	Zephaniah	1 Corinthians 8
227.	Haggai	1 Corinthians 9
228.	Zechariah 1–4	1 Corinthians 10
229.	Zechariah 5–9	1 Corinthians 11
230.	Zechariah 10–14	1 Corinthians 12

231.	**Reflect**

232.	Malachi	1 Corinthians 13
233.	Psalms 1–6	1 Corinthians 14
234.	Psalms 7–11	1 Corinthians 15:1-20
235.	Psalms 12–17	1 Corinthians 15:21-58
236.	Psalms 18–19	1 Corinthians 16
237.	Psalms 20–22	2 Corinthians 1

238.	**Reflect**

239.	Psalms 23–27	2 Corinthians 2
240.	Psalms 28–31	2 Corinthians 3
241.	Psalms 32–35	2 Corinthians 4
242.	Psalms 36–38	2 Corinthians 5
243.	Psalms 39–41	2 Corinthians 6
244.	Psalms 42–44	2 Corinthians 7

245.	**Reflect**

246.	Psalms 45–47	2 Corinthians 8
247.	Psalms 48–50	2 Corinthians 9
248.	Psalm 51	2 Corinthians 10
249.	Psalms 52–55	2 Corinthians 11
250.	Psalms 56–59	2 Corinthians 12
251.	Psalms 60–64	2 Corinthians 13

252.	**Reflect**

253.	Psalms 65–67	Galatians 1
254.	Psalms 68–69	Galatians 2

255. Psalms 70–72	Galatians 3
256. Psalms 73–74	Galatians 4
257. Psalms 75–77	Galatians 5
258. Psalm 78	Galatians 6

259. Reflect

260. Psalms 79–81	Ephesians 1
261. Psalms 82–86	Ephesians 2
262. Psalms 87–89	Ephesians 3
263. Psalms 90–93	Ephesians 4
264. Psalms 94–97	Ephesians 5
265. Psalms 98–102	Ephesians 6

266. Reflect

267. Psalms 103–104	Philippians 1
268. Psalms 105–106	Philippians 2
269. Psalms 107–108	Philippians 3
270. Psalms 109–110	Philippians 4
271. Psalms 111–114	Colossians 1
272. Psalms 115–118	Colossians 2

273. Reflect

274. Psalm 119:1-56	Colossians 3
275. Psalm 119:57-112	Colossians 4
276. Psalm 119:113-176	1 Thessalonians 1
277. Psalms 120–126	1 Thessalonians 2
278. Psalms 127–134	1 Thessalonians 3
279. Psalms 135–136	1 Thessalonians 4

280. Reflect

281. Psalms 137–140	1 Thessalonians 5
282. Psalms 141–144	2 Thessalonians 1
283. Psalms 145–147	2 Thessalonians 2
284. Psalms 148–150	2 Thessalonians 3
285. Job 1–2	1 Timothy 1
286. Job 3–5	1 Timothy 2

287. Reflect

288.	Job 6–8	1 Timothy 3
289.	Job 9–11	1 Timothy 4
290.	Job 12–14	1 Timothy 5
291.	Job 15–17	1 Timothy 6
292.	Job 18–19	2 Timothy 1
293.	Job 20–22	2 Timothy 2

294. Reflect

295.	Job 23–25	2 Timothy 3
296.	Job 26–28	2 Timothy 4
297.	Job 29–31	Titus 1
298.	Job 32–34	Titus 2
299.	Job 35–37	Titus 3
300.	Job 38–42	Philemon

301. Reflect

302.	Proverbs 1–3	Hebrews 1
303.	Proverbs 4–6	Hebrews 2–3
304.	Proverbs 7–9	Hebrews 4:1–5:10
305.	Proverbs 10–12	Hebrews 5:11–6:20
306.	Proverbs 13–15	Hebrews 7–8
307.	Proverbs 16–18	Hebrews 9

308. Reflect

309.	Proverbs 19–21	Hebrews 10
310.	Proverbs 22–24	Hebrews 11
311.	Proverbs 25–27	Hebrews 12
312.	Proverbs 28–31	Hebrews 13
313.	Ruth	James 1
314.	Song of Songs 1–3	James 2

315. Reflect

316.	Song of Songs 4–8	James 3
317.	Ecclesiastes 1–3	James 4
318.	Ecclesiastes 4–7	James 5
319.	Ecclesiastes 8–12	1 Peter 1
320.	Lamentations 1–2	1 Peter 2
321.	Lamentations 3–5	1 Peter 3

322.	**Reflect**	
323.	Esther 1–2	1 Peter 4
324.	Esther 3–6	1 Peter 5
325.	Esther 7–10	2 Peter 1
326.	Daniel 1–2	2 Peter 2
327.	Daniel 3–6	2 Peter 3
328.	Daniel 7–9	1 John 1
329.	**Reflect**	
330.	Daniel 10–12	1 John 2
331.	Ezra 1–3	1 John 3
332.	Ezra 4–6	1 John 4
333.	Ezra 7–10	1 John 5
334.	Nehemiah 1–3	2 John
335.	Nehemiah 4–6	3 John
336.	**Reflect**	
337.	Nehemiah 7–9	Jude
338.	Nehemiah 10–13	Revelation 1
339.	1 Chronicles 1–5	Revelation 2:1-17
340.	1 Chronicles 6–9	Revelation 2:18–3:6
341.	1 Chronicles 10–12	Revelation 3:7-22
342.	1 Chronicles 13–15	Revelation 4
343.	**Reflect**	
344.	1 Chronicles 16–18	Revelation 5
345.	1 Chronicles 19–22	Revelation 6
346.	1 Chronicles 23–26	Revelation 7
347.	1 Chronicles 27–29	Revelation 8
348.	2 Chronicles 1–3	Revelation 9
349.	2 Chronicles 4–6	Revelation 10
350.	**Reflect**	
351.	2 Chronicles 7–9	Revelation 11
352.	2 Chronicles 10–12	Revelation 12
353.	2 Chronicles 13–14	Revelation 13
354.	2 Chronicles 15–16	Revelation 14

| 355. | 2 Chronicles 17–18 | Revelation 15 |
| 356. | 2 Chronicles 19–20 | Revelation 16 |

357. Reflect

358.	2 Chronicles 21–23	Revelation 17
359.	2 Chronicles 24–25	Revelation 18
360.	2 Chronicles 26–28	Revelation 19
361.	2 Chronicles 29–31	Revelation 20
362.	2 Chronicles 32–33	Revelation 21
363.	2 Chronicles 34–36	Revelation 22

364. Reflect

365. Reflect upon the year

A SCHEDULE TO READ THROUGH THE BIBLE IN ONE MONTH

APPENDIX B

1. Genesis 1–39

2. Genesis 40–Exodus 28

3. Exodus 29–Leviticus

4. Numbers–Deuteronomy 3

5. Deuteronomy 4–Joshua 8

6. Joshua 9–Judges 13

7. Judges 14–21; 1 Samuel 1–21

8. 1 Samuel 22–1 Kings 5

9. 1 Kings 6–2 Kings 22

10. 2 Kings 23–25; Isaiah 1–35

11. Isaiah 36–Jeremiah 8

12. Jeremiah 9–47

13. Jeremiah 48–52; Ezekiel 1–34

14. Ezekiel 35–48; Hosea; Joel; Amos; Obadiah

15. Jonah–Malachi

16. Psalms 1–41

17. Psalms 42–72

18. Psalms 73–106

19. Psalms 107–150

20. Job

21. Proverbs

22. Ruth; Song of Songs; Ecclesiastes; Lamentations; Esther

23. Daniel; Ezra; Nehemiah

24. 1 Chronicles 1–2 Chronicles 10

25. 2 Chronicles 11–36; Matthew 1–13

26. Matthew 14–Luke 8

27. Luke 9–Acts 23

28. Acts 24–2 Corinthians 7

29. 2 Corinthians 8–2 Thessalonians

30. 1 Timothy–James

31. 1 Peter–Revelation

NOTES

1. Andy Park, "In the Secret" (Mercy/Vineyard, 1995).
2. Although a 1937 issue of *Reader's Digest* attributed this quote to Mark Twain, it cannot be found anywhere else.
3. Michael Crichton, *Jurassic Park* (New York: Knopf, 1990), 286.
4. Francis A. Schaeffer, *How Should We Then Live?* (Westchester, IL: Crossway, 1976), 138.
5. Frank Newport, "Twenty-Eight Percent Believe Bible Is Actual Word of God," *The Gallup Poll*, May 22, 2006, http://poll.gallup.com/content/?ci=22885.
6. http://roswell.tobaccodocuments.org/pollay/dirdet.cfm? DispResults=yes&Brand=Julep&Format=Advertisement &Company=&ProductType=Cigarette&searchString=& startDate=&endDate=&OrderBy=Brand&bibCode=& Search=Search.
7. Richard Foster, *Celebration of Discipline: The Path to Spiritual Growth* (San Francisco: HarperSanFrancisco, 1998), 135.
8. Paul Johnson, *Creators: From Chaucer and Dürer to Picasso and Disney* (New York: HarperCollins, 2006), 1.

9. *Seinfeld*. Episode no. 109, first broadcast 11 May 1995 by NBC. Directed by Andy Ackerman and written by Larry David.

10. *ABC News*, "'Death by Alcohol' Warns of College Binge Drinking Risks," *Good Morning America*, June 12, 2006, http://www.abcnews.go.com/GMA/Health/story?id=2065494&page=1.

11. Higher Education Research Institute study cited by Ed Vitagliano in "A Strange Faith—Are Church-Going Kids Christian?" *AgapePress*, November 15, 2005, http://headlines.agapepress.org/archive/11/152005a.asp.

12. Sigmund Freud, *New Introductory Lectures on Psycho-Analysis*, ed. Joan Riviere (London: Hogarth Press, 1933), 97.

13. C. S. Lewis, *Mere Christianity* (San Francisco: HarperSanFrancisco, 2001), 24.

14. Brooke Foss Westcott, *The Gospel According to St. John* (London: John Murray, 1882), 228.

15. Joan Didion, "The Case of Theresa Schiavo," *The New York Review of Books*, June 9, 2005.

16. William Barclay, *The Revelation of John* (Edinburgh: St. Andrew Press, 2004), 1:107.

ABOUT THE AUTHOR

MARK is the author of more than a dozen books, including *Living with Less: The Upside of Downsizing Your Life* (Broadman & Holman), *Greater Than: Unconventional Thoughts on the Infinite God* (TH1NK), and the 2004 Gold Medallion finalist *Out of the Whirlwind* (Broadman & Holman). His collaborative works include *The Unusual Suspect* with Stephen Baldwin (FaithWords) and *Strike Zone* with Andy Pettitte (Broadman & Holman). Mark is also general editor of TH1NK's STUDENT REFERENCE LIBRARY. In addition to his work as a writer, Mark is a volunteer firefighter and serves as chaplain for his local fire department. He and his family and their two dachshunds live in Indiana. To learn more, visit his website, www.marktabb.com.

ABOUT THE DISCUSSION GUIDE WRITER

GREG LIPPS, mild-mannered visitor from another planet . . . no . . . wait, that's classified.

Greg Lipps is a father of five from Greenfield, Indiana. He has two grandchildren and more pets than he cares to mention.

He holds a degree and various certifications in Computer Technology and works full time for AT&T as a Senior Technical Team Lead for computer systems development. He held various leadership positions for the Boy Scouts for ten years and has been a youth-ministry leader, Sunday-school teacher, home-group leader, and all around church flunky for more than twenty years. He is a member of Brandywine Community Church in Greenfield.

MORE GREAT BOOKS FOR FINDING A FAITH ALL YOUR OWN.

What You Didn't Learn from Your Parents About Christianity

Matthew Paul Turner 1-57683-942-7

Popular author Matthew Paul Turner presents a unique reference guide to the basics of the Christian faith, providing foundational truths and practical insights that are infused with his knowing wit and honesty.

How to Stay Christian in College

J. Budziszewski 1-57683-510-3

Going away to college can be exciting, scary, wild, or all of the above. This guide lets you know what to expect and examines different worldviews and myths you may encounter at school. Filled with anecdotes, resources, and much more, it will prepare, equip, and encourage you to meet the challenge of living out your faith at school.

Redefining Life (Identity)

TH1NK Books 1-57683-828-5

So, who are you? Only you can know. And part of the journey of self-discovery is God-discovery because He's the One who fashioned you. There is freedom in knowing who you are, and this discussion guide will help with the process. You'll not only discover what you were created for but also learn about the One who created you.